永和九年歲在癸丑暮春之初會于會稽山陰之蘭亭修禊事也群賢畢至少長咸集此地有崇山峻嶺茂林修竹又有清流激湍映帶左右引以為流觴曲水列坐其次雖無絲竹管絃之盛一觴一詠亦足以暢敘幽情是日也天朗氣清惠風和暢仰觀宇宙之大俯察品類之盛所以遊目騁懷足以極視聽之娛信可

Endpapers show a close up detail of number 251

An Exhibition of

Chinese Snuff Bottles from the Collection of Mary and George Bloch

at the Galleries of

Sydney L. Moss, Ltd.
51 Brook Street
London W1

Monday, 12th October to Friday, 23rd October, 1987

Catalogue by
Robert W.L. Kleiner

Credits

Photography:
Maggie Nimkin
New York

Watercolours:
Peter Suart
Hong Kong

Translations:
Regina Krahl
Nyr Indictor

Design:
Robert W.L. Kleiner
Pressroom Printer & Designer

Printer:
Pressroom Printer & Designer
37 Wellington Street
604 Red A Central Building
Central
Hong Kong

Catalogues available from:
Herald International Ltd.
8th Floor
Wing On Life Building
22 Des Voeux Road Central
Hong Kong

ISBN 962-7287-01-6
First Printing: 1987

Foreword

Collecting has the same potential for self-realization and self-expression as an art form as has any other creative activity, and in a quarter of a century of dealing with collectors I have seldom seen that potential more fully realized than with the Blochs.

Mary and George Bloch collect like Picasso painted, with clarity of vision, certainty of purpose, dedication and prolific creativity. The result has been quite extraordinary. In a very short period of time they have formed what must now rank as one of the world's finest collections of Chinese snuff bottles. To have formed such a collection in the time frame measured in decades to which snuff bottle collectors are accustomed would have been a considerable achievement. To have done so in less than five years, starting without any knowledge of the field at all, represents, in collecting terms, a creative masterpiece.

Nor is this their only collecting interest. They have also formed, over a much longer period of time, a major collection of modern Western painting and sculpture. As I write, a selection from this collection is on exhibition at the Hong Kong Museum of Art, where the works of Picasso, Moore, Miro, Dubuffet, Degas, George Rouault, Barbara Hepworth, Archipenko and others delight the eye of the Hong Kong public as they have so often delighted mine at the Bloch's home.

It may seem a strange progression from the height of modern Western art — perceived as the most profound expression of what is arguably one of the greatest revolutions in consciousness in Western history — to Chinese snuff bottles, which have so often been seen as no more than the trinkets of craftsmanship.

However, such a view of art, seeking as it does to establish a hierarchy of profundity based primarily upon the art object, is in ironic contradiction to the very nature of the modern revolution in Western art. In China such objectivity has never governed aesthetics. Thus any objective hierarchy applied to comparisons between the two art forms that are the core of the Bloch's collecting activities is rendered meaningless.

Although Oriental arts are now widely collected in the West a clear perspective that reveals the whole pattern of world art is, for the vast majority, absent. Ethnocentricity still tends to colour art appreciation to a confusing degree. I believe a useful key to this problem is provided by recognizing a distinction between Objective and Subjective Aesthetics, and the collecting interests of the Blochs provides a useful opportunity to explore this idea.

Objective Aesthetics, which has governed Western art for many centuries until our modern revolution in perception and therefore in expression, tends to see the art objects as the end product of art. The artist is seen as dealing, through vision, with a higher order of meaning, which is then translated, through technique, into a physical work of art of some kind, but there the 'art' stops. The audience is then perceived as quite separate from the work of art, placing the main emphasis, thereby, upon the art object itself. Meaning is sought at its surface.

Today this causes very considerable confusion, as art is no longer following the rules of Objective Aesthetics, while the audience, too often still clings to a tradition it has been heir to for centuries and with which it is comfortable. The significance of much that is currently presented as art is, therefore, largely lost on the audience.

Subjective Aesthetics, which has always governed in China (the concept of silence as the purest form of music, for instance, was already established at the time of Confucius two and a half thousand years before John Cage introduced it for the West), goes much further. It is not an alternative to objective Aesthetics, but includes it — as the Universe includes our planet, and Quantum Mechanics includes Newtonian Physics. It is simply a broader perspective.

Subjective Aesthetics does not emphasize the product of art but the whole process. It recognizes the meaning/vision/technique/object progression of Objective Aesthetics but instead of stopping there continues through audience techniques, audience vision, and eventually audience perception in perceiving higher meaning. The end 'product' of art is enlightenment, higher understanding, the evolution of consciousness, not the work of art itself.

In Subjective Aesthetics art is seen as a process not a product, as a path to higher understanding on which the art object is a signpost along the way; as one of our many creative means of pursuing what is ultimately our only serious concern, which is the evolution of human consciousness.

This de-emphasizes the physical work of art; removes the need to specifically understand what the artist or the work of art 'means' and involves the audience fully (and without a set of no-longer-appropriate, and therefore thoroughly confusing rules) in one of the most delightful, creative romps towards enlightenment open to us.

We, the audience, become full partners in the artistic process; our perspective is radically changed and with it the whole landscape of art. Physical distinctions and objective hierarchies (music, painting and sculpture are 'Fine' arts; pottery, rug-making and carpentry are crafts; Bach is necessarily more profound than David Bowie, etc.) become no more than the analogical structures we build in order to *communicate* experience, further signposts along the way. They may point us in the right direction, from the particular and therefore relative point at which we may find ourselves (as does a physical work of art) but they have no real meaning independent of the whole process of artistic communication.

From the relatively limited viewpoint of Objective Aesthetics we are able to believe that there are rules which govern art, while Subjective Aesthetics demonstrates that rules arise out of art but do not govern it — they are a function of communication *about* art, not of art itself. Similarly, Newtonian Physics allowed us to believe that the Universe was a massive mechanism, constructed of independent parts, while Quantum Mechanics demonstrates that at the sub-atomic level what we are dealing with is not separate parts, but an infinitely complex web of inseparable patterns of energy which include the consciousness of the human observer of this extraordinary cosmic 'dance'. As consciousness evolves, our new levels of understanding are similarly breaking down the traditional distinctions between different disciplines. Physicists find themselves dealing with remarkably similar areas of consideration as ancient Oriental philosophers, medicine and mysticism begin to flirt in a manner unthinkable a generation ago, etc.

The Blochs, unlike so many collectors of modern Western art, have fully grasped the meaning of its modernism. They are ruled by no illusory hierarchies (while recogizing their relative role), and in devoting the same seriousness of attention to a Ding Erzhong as they do to a Picasso, to an Imperial ivory snuff bottle as to an Archipenko or a Henry Moore sculpture — in seeing past the products to the process — they are at the same time pioneers of modern aesthetics (although in China such 'modernism' is measured in millenia) and in a very real sense, artists.

Over the past few years, as I have been happily drawn into their creative effort, I have enjoyed many lengthy discussions on the subject in an attempt to understand conceptually the manifestation of an apparently intuitive need which has swept the Western world in the past century.

That need has made of aesthetics a source of spiritual meaning for our age once largely the domain of religion.

Tolstoy in the 1880's foresaw this shift of emphasis from religion to a new form of spiritual meaning, although he left it nameless, and we see it today in the massive international awakening of interest in the arts, and in the gradual emergence of new art forms that are ever more all-encompassing, culminating in the ancient Oriental perception of life as the ultimate art form in which all other arts are subsumed. At which point no profound distinction exists between meditation, philosophy, art, or any of our other myriad means of refining our understanding towards a point of 'perfect' understanding. (Which, of course also raises the need for an expanded meaning for the word Aesthetics to deal with the new levels of consciousness; one that includes all aspects of the way in which we creatively perceive and express experience — so much of art terminology is in need of expansion to cope with the new Aesthetics, including the term itself!)

This is the perspective from which I delight in both the creative breadth of Mary and George Bloch's achievement and the friendship that both invites me, and prompts me to write this foreword, making it pertinent to stray so far from the traditional stomping ground of the writer on snuff bottles into the realm of art theory and the aesthetics of appreciation.

Hugh Moss

At the Water, Pine and Stone Retreat,
Hong Kong, April, 1987

Introduction

This catalogue contains a selection of 310 snuff bottles from a collection of nearly 800 formed by Mary and George Bloch. The aim of the catalogue is to provide as complete a view as possible of the scope and range of the snuff bottle, from its earliest beginnings in the Shunzhi period (1644-1661), to its most recent flowering, the inside-painted bottles by Wang Xisan achieved as late as the 1960's and 1970's.

Rather than writing a specific chapter about each group, such as enamelled bottles or inside-painted bottles, I have written a commentary for each bottle which both relates to that particular bottle and adds some background information on the group to which it belongs. Thus if one takes the first section of twenty-three enamelled bottles and reads each commentary consecutively one should, as one progresses, gradually acquire information about the group as a whole so that when the final bottle has been reached one will have built up a fairly complete feeling for that group.

Such an approach is only possible with a collection of the highest quality, in which each section of bottles contains sufficient examples to illustrate all, or most of the points that need to be made about that group.

In this respect, the achievement of Mary and George Bloch is unparalleled. They have succeeded in bringing together so many examples of varieties within each particular field that these not only serve to illustrate much of the known ambit of that group but also inevitably add to one's knowledge.

Thus, for instance, if one studies the inside-painted bottles by Ding Erzhong in this catalogue one is presented with a unique opportunity. The works of this particular artist are so rare that, in general, if one wishes to study them one has to be content with examining one or two examples, or perhaps a handful of photographs. Yet, here we have thirteen examples, ranging from his earliest work to his most mature, all illustrated together in one flowing sweep. Taken as such, a feeling for Ding's overall style and technique can be acquired in a manner never before possible. One begins to notice the way in which he paints the foliage of the trees or constructs the landscape backgrounds, and perhaps even more exciting, one can observe his development as an artist, his growing confidence in this medium and his exploration of new ways of stating the same theme; a rose growing from bud to full bloom before our eyes.

A further advantage of this approach is that one can begin to discern links between different groups so that a pointer to the dating or place of manufacture of, for instance a glass bottle, might help in the dating of a jade bottle.

Thus we have the enamelled glass bottle, number 15, which is unquestionably of the period of Qianlong (1736-1795) and undoubtedly made in the Palace Workshops in Beijing, and we can observe an almost identical reign-mark on the jade bottle (number 24), the glass bottles, (numbers 63-65) the ivory bottles (numbers 187, 190 and 191) and the turquoise bottle (number 174). Such links would be much more difficult to discern if each of these bottles had been viewed individually over a period of time.

Similarly, it may be possible to see the same hand at work in the two Suzhou chalcedony bottles, (numbers 149 and 150), or in the two chalcedony bottles, numbers 166 and 168.

DATING

The question of dating is particularly difficult in the field of snuff bottles. Where the bottle possesses a reign mark or a princely hall mark it is possible to date it accurately by simply comparing its style and characteristics with similarly marked documented works of art. Thus the Qianlong-marked examples of enamelled wares, glass and porcelain may all be compared with their counterparts in the great repositories of such documented wares in Taiwan, Beijing or the West. The wares belonging to Prince Ding, Zaichuan, from the Hall of Constancy (*Xingyouheng Tang*) are equally well documented (see number 141).

However, when we examine the great majority of snuff bottles, which do not possess incontrovertable clues such as a reign mark, the question of dating becomes more subjective. One must continue to compare the style and characteristics of such bottles with similar documented examples but it becomes more difficult to be categorical about, for instance, a particular reign as a period of manufacture. Thus, rather than stating that a particular item dates from the Qianlong reign (1736-1795), it is often more accurate to state that it dates from 1750 to 1820, or 1780 to 1850. This is particularly so of the vast majority of chalcedony bottles, but much less so with the jade bottles, which can more easily be compared with the very large number of well documented, but largely unmarked jade artifacts which were made during the eighteenth century.

It is possible that collectors place too much importance on the date of manufacture of an item and thus tend to overlook its intrinsic artistic merit. In this connection, the real value of this catalogue lies in the superb quality of the illustrations. These are very nearly the equivalent of holding the actual object in one's hand, and the reader thus has the opportunity to do his own studying. The commentaries provide a guide, but it is up to the beholder to use his own eyes and observe.

Looked at from this point of view, a simple and not very valuable bottle, such as the porcelain example, number 235, is arguably as great a work of art as the vastly more valuable and rare enamelled bottle, number 2. From an objective point of view there is no comparison. The enamelled bottle is far more beautiful, required far more skill to achieve and has a far grander provenance. It is the best of its type. And yet the porcelain bottle is also the best of its type, a type made in immensely greater numbers than was the enamelled bottle. Very few enamelled bottles were made and they are all superb. The great majority of porcelain bottles are almost all mediocre or worse, but here we have one which has risen above the great mass, because for one moment the craftsman, whose job it was to turn out bottle after bottle of the same design, was inspired to rise above himself, forget his conventions and paint what he felt.

Thus a bottle, which most connoisseurs would immediately ignore because of its humble orgins, reveals itself, after a little study, as an exciting work of art and for this reason alone it deserves a place in the catalcgue.

It is hoped that this catalogue will form the basis of a book on the complete collection of Mary and George Bloch in which it will be possible to publish actual illustrations of comparative material wherever possible, rather than citing references in footnotes.

I would like to thank Mary and George Bloch for so freely making available their magnificent collection for study, and for all their support and encouragement during the germination of the catalogue. It is rare that a writer in any field has such a stimulating and fine body of material from which to work. In this connection, it has been a profound privilege and pleasure helping and advising Mary and George in the building of the collection, and the type of opportunity of which most 'experts' in any particular field can only dream. I would also like to thank Hugh Moss for his many helpful comments at the proof stage, Maggie Nimkin for her superb photographs, which are the best I have ever seen of snuff bottles, my Father for his help in research, Desirée Bucks and her staff at Pressroom for their tireless enthusiasm, Regina Krahl and Nyr Indictor for their translations and many members of staff at Sotheby's who have helped with the mechanics of getting the catalogue to press.

Robert Kleiner
Sotheby's
September 1987

Enamels on Copper

 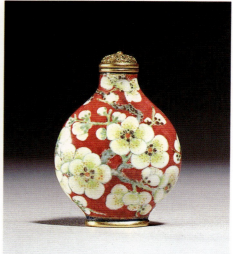

1

Painted enamels on copper; polychrome; with a continuous design of blossoming prunus on a ruby-red ground, the base inscribed in blue *Kangxi yuzhi (made by imperial order of the Kangxi Emperor); height: 5.1cm.*

Beijing Palace Workshops; 1715-1722

    PROVENANCE: Hugh Moss
                        The Belfort Collection

    EXHIBITED: Arcade Chaumet, Paris, June 1982, *Catalogue*, no. 247

This bottle, which is one of the earliest known examples of Chinese enamel ware, has a gold foot applied, probably because of the poor definition of the original foot, due to the experimental nature of the enamelling process at this date.

According to Matteo Ripa enamelled metal wares were first painted in the Beijing Palace Workshops at some time before 1716[1]. The Kangxi Emperor took a close interest in these wares and the group, which includes bowls, incense burners, small vases and snuff bottles all bear the imperial command *yuzhi* mark, rather than the more usual *nianzhi* mark.

The form *yuzhi* ranks high in the hierarchy of imperial marks. At the lower end of the scale come the six character marks which include the name of the dynasty. Above these is the four character designation *nianzhi* (made in the year of); this form was widely used in the Palace Workshops. Then comes the group which use the form *yuzhi*, (imperially made). These indicate that the emperor took a particular interest in their production, although it did not imply that the items were for his sole use. Above these comes a series of marks such as *yuwan, yuyong* and *shangwan* which imply a personal use by the emperor himself[2].

A *yuzhi*-marked bowl with almost identical decoration to that of this snuff bottle is in the British Museum (ref.1939.10.14.1)[3], and a Canton enamel version with a Yongzheng mark has been recorded[4].

Only eight snuff bottles with the *yuzhi* mark have been recorded, including two in the National Palace Museum, Taiwan[5].

1. *Memoirs of Father Ripa during thirteen years residence at the court of Peking.* Selected and translated from the Italian by F. Prandix, London 1844.
2. G. Tsang and H. Moss. *Arts From the Scholar's Studio*, no. 130.
3. H. Moss. *By Imperial Command*, pl. 10.
4. Yang Boda. *Tributes From Guangdong to the Qing Court*, p. 34, fig 6.
5. *Masterpieces of Chinese Snuff Bottles, in the National Palace Museum, Taiwan*, pl. 26.

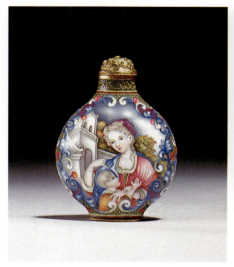 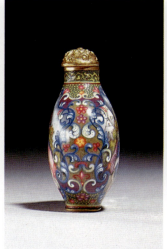 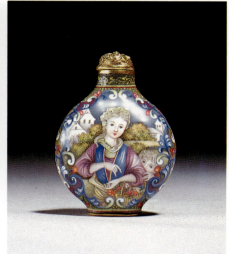

2

Painted enamels on copper; polychrome; with a panel on each side illustrating an elaborately dressed European lady and a small boy, with buildings in the background, the shoulders with interlaced scrolls on an olive-green ground, the base inscribed in blue *Qianlong nianzhi* (*made in the Qianlong period*); *height: 4.5cm.*

Beijing Palace Workshops; 1736-1795

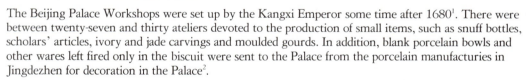

    PROVENANCE: A.W. Bahr
                         R.H. Ellsworth
                         Christies, New York, 9th May 1981, lot 419
                         Hugh Moss
                         Dr. Paula Hallett

The Beijing Palace Workshops were set up by the Kangxi Emperor some time after 1680[1]. There were between twenty-seven and thirty ateliers devoted to the production of small items, such as snuff bottles, scholars' articles, ivory and jade carvings and moulded gourds. In addition, blank porcelain bowls and other wares left fired only in the biscuit were sent to the Palace from the porcelain manufactures in Jingdezhen for decoration in the Palace[2].

These workshops flourished throughout the eighteenth century, encouraged successively by the Kangxi, Yongzheng and Qianlong Emperors, and various sources depict the degree of imperial patronage involved[3]. The workshops went into a decline in the nineteenth century, however with fewer and fewer good examples being produced (for a possible exception to this trend see the Guangxu-marked glass bottle no. 83 in this exhibition which dates from the late nineteenth century).

The three eighteenth century Emperors were all fascinated by European culture and went to great lengths to have the numerous Jesuit missionaries[4], who were attached to the court, teach local craftsmen the techniques of enamelling.

European subjects were favoured, particularly a series of prettily dressed young girls, possibly by the same hand as the artist of this bottle, which are depicted on numerous vases and boxes in the National Palace Museum, Taiwan[5]. (Compare, in addition, the enamelled glass bottle, no. 12 in this catalogue).

1. G. Tsang and H. Moss. *Arts From the Scholar's Studio*, no 91.
2. H. Moss. *By Imperial Command*, *passim*.
3. Kao Shigi records a retirement gift to himself from the Kangxi Emperor in 1703 (See G. Tsang, *op. cit* in footnote no. 4 to the bronze bottle, number 244 below).
4. 'Missionery Artists at the Manchu Court'. G. Loehr, T.O.C.S., 12th June 1963.
5. *Illustrated Catalogue of Ch'ing Dynasty Porcelain in the National Palace Museum, Republic of China.* 'Chienlung and other wares', pls. 53, 54 & 72.

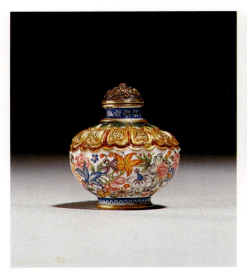
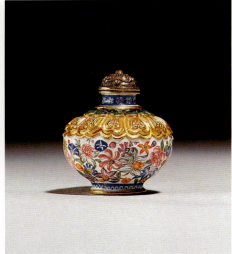

3

Painted enamels on gold; polychrome; with a continuous ''mille-fleurs'' design of lilies and exotic plants on a white ground, the shoulders carved with a petal-lappet border bearing traces of red enamel beneath a border of smaller green enamelled petals, the base inscribed in blue *Qianlong nianzhi* (*made in the Qianlong period*); *height: 3.2cm*.

Beijing Palace Workshops; 1736-1795

PROVENANCE:	Hugh Moss
	The Belfort Collection
EXHIBITED:	Hong Kong Museum of Art, October 1978
PUBLISHED:	H. Moss. *By Imperial Command*, pl. 30
	Hong Kong Museum of Art. 'Snuff Bottles of the Ch'ing Dynasty', *Catalogue*, no. 11
	V Jutheau. *Journal* of the I.C.S.B.S., December, 1975, p. 8, no. 21

Enamelled bottles on a gold ground are of outstanding rarety, only three having been recorded. The reason for this could be the extra difficulty caused by the medium itself, the gold being far less able to retain the enamelled covering than the more commonly used copper.

A Qianlong vessel and stand with an identical 'mille-fleurs' design is in the National Palace Museum, Taiwan[1].

1. *Masterpieces of Chinese Enamelled Ware, in the National Palace Museum, Taiwan*, pl. 35.

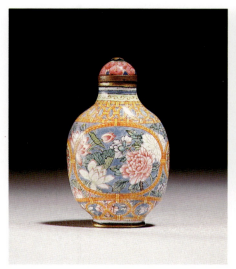  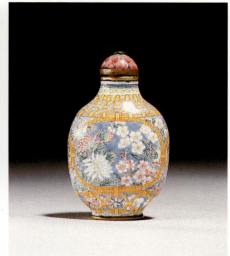

4

Painted enamels on copper; polychrome; with a continuous scene of lotus, peony, chrysanthemum and prunus on a pale blue stippled ground, enclosed by ropework borders forming interlaced cash around the shoulders and foot, the shoulders with small dragon medallions, the base inscribed in blue *Qianlong nianzhi* (*made in the Qianlong period*); height: 4.5cm.

Beijing Palace Workshops; 1736-1795

PROVENANCE: Hugh Moss
Blair L. Hills

EXHIBITED: Hong Kong Museum of Art, October 1978

PUBLISHED: Hong Kong Museum. *Catalogue*, no. 12

The Chinese have always been devoted to the culture and love of flowers and the flowers on this bottle represent the four seasons; the peony for spring; the lotus for summer; the chrysanthemum for autumn; and the prunus for winter[1].

Ropework borders appear often on items made in the Palace Workshops.

1. C.A.S. Williams. *Outlines of Chinese Symbolism and Art Motifs.*

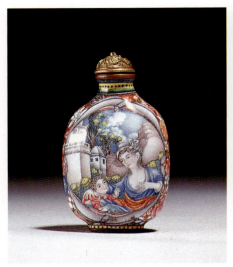  

5

Painted enamels on copper; polychrome; with a slightly differing panel on each side depicting a European lady, one *en décolletée*, each with a child, buildings in the background, the shoulders with a richly painted 'mille-fleurs' design, the base inscribed in blue *Qianlong nianzhi*, (*made in the Qianlong period*); *height 5.2cm*.

Beijing Palace Workshops; 1736-1795

    PROVENANCE: Hugh Moss
                        The Belfort Collection

    PUBLISHED: V. Jutheau. *Journal* of the I.C.S.B.S., March 1975

This bottle exhibits a minute pattern of faint cracks, which occurs because of the difficulty in maintaining perfect control over the firing of the enamels. The copper bodies for the bottles were probably provided by the atelier responsible for cloisonné enamel production. These bodies were then covered in a white enamel which was fired, covered again and refired several times until a reasonable thickness was achieved. Subsequently the coloured designs were added and in the later re-firing a contraction of the outer enamels sometimes took place resulting in the faint cracks which are visible in this case[1].

With regard to the plunging neckline of one of the ladies depicted on this bottle the interesting point has been made that such a subject would not have emanated from the Palace Workshops as the Qianlong Emperor did not tolerate such subject-matter[2].

However this argument cannot withstand a closer analysis on two counts. First the quality of the painting is of the highest order. Therefore if it was not created in the Palace Workshops it must have been made in Guangzhou, the only other centre of enamelling in China. If it had been made in Guangzhou, it is so far superior to the other products of the Guangzhou Workshops that it would have been intended as a Court Tribute[3]. If it was intended as a court tribute it would have been seen by the Emperor in any event. The second count is that the painting of the ladies on this bottle and the 'mille-fleurs' background compare so closely to that of the palace-enamelled wares discussed above[4], and to those in the National Palace Museum and the Percival David Collection, London, that there can be no doubt as to its palace origin.

1. H. Moss. *By Imperial Command*, p. 46.
2. E.B. Curtis. 'The Impact of the West', *Journal* of the I.C.S.B.S., Winter 1983.
3. For a further discussion of the Guangzhou Workshops see number 9 below.
4. See numbers 2 and 3.

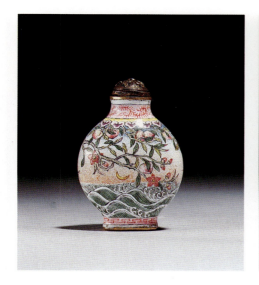

6
_____

Painted enamels on copper; polychrome; with a continuous scene depicting a fruiting peach tree growing from a rock rising from a sea of crested waves, a bat swooping to one side with the crescent moon and the sun in the sky, the base inscribed in blue *Qianlong nianzhi (made in the Qianlong period),* written in a line; *height: 4.2cm.*

Beijing Palace Workshops; 1736-1795

PROVENANCE: Honor Smith
Hugh Moss
Dr. Paula Hallett
Sotheby's, New York, 2nd December 1985, lot 43

PUBLISHED: *Journal* of the I.C.S.B.S., December 1975, p. 8, fig 22

The peach has an important place in Chinese culture and is the emblem of marriage and longevity. Its wood and its colour keep demons away, and its petals would cast spells over men[1].

1. Wolfram Eberhard. *A Dictionary of Chinese Symbols.*

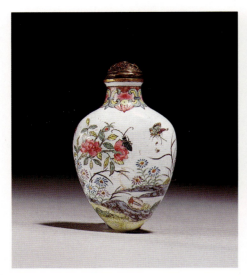

7

Painted enamels on copper; polychrome; with a continuous scene depicting bees and butterflies hovering above clusters of peony and daisy springing from rocks and a mossy bank, an elaborate collar of interlaced 'C'-shaped motifs around the neck; *height: 4.8cm*.

Beijing Palace Workshops; Qianlong period, 1736-1795

      PROVENANCE: Honor Smith
                        Hugh Moss
                        Dr. Paula Hallett
                        Sotheby's, New York, 2nd December 1985, lot 43

This bottle is unusual in that its flattened pear shape does not allow any space for the identifying reign mark. Nevertheless a close study of the style of painting leaves no doubt as to either its period or its place of manufacture in Beijing.

The rockwork is skilfully shaded as are the petals of the flowers and these features compare very closely with similar features both on marked palace enamel bottles and on imperial porcelains with similar subject matter. The composition is well balanced and fluid throughout, the artist exhibiting confidence and control with a difficult shape to fill.

The actual technique of painting, common to all the enamel bottles attributed to Beijing, involves the minute stippling of the background as is apparent in the green of the mossy bank around the base. In addition, the elaborate collar, which compares closely to that on the enamelled glass bottle, no. 13 in this catalogue and to numerous examples in the National Palace Museum[1], is not a style found on bottles enamelled in Guangzhou.

This bottle and no. 6 above both came together in a specially fitted box of some age, inscribed on the lid 'Qianlong imperial snuff bottles'.

1. Lin-sheng Chang. 'Enamel painted bottles of the Ch'ing Dynasty', *Journal* of the I.C.S.B.S., March 1979.

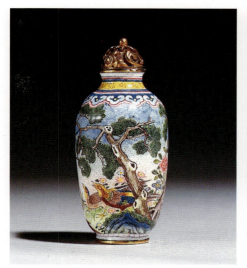

8
___

Painted enamels on copper; polychrome; with a continuous scene depicting a pheasant and its mate looking up at a cluster of yellow-throated birds perched in a pine tree, with numerous flowers springing from a mossy bank and rocks, a *ruyi*-head and key-fret border on the shoulders, the base inscribed in blue *Qianlong nianzhi (made in the Qianlong period)*; *height: 5.6cm*.

Beijing Palace Workshops; 1790-1795

    PROVENANCE: The Ko Collection

This bottle bears a striking similarity to one in the Eugene Fuller Memorial Collection, The Seattle Art Museum, Washington, U.S.A.[1]. The Seattle bottle bears the reign mark of the Jiaqing Emperor, who reigned from 1796-1820, and it is therefore reasonable to assume that the Qianlong example above, which was almost certainly painted by the same hand, must date from very late in the Qianlong reign, which ended in 1795.

Another bottle by the same hand, bearing the mark *Qianlong yuzhi*, which is the only recorded example on an enamel snuff bottle of this particular form in the Qianlong reign, (from the collection of Charles V Swain) is illustrated in the Exhibition *Catalogue*, 'Snuff Bottles of the Ch'ing Dynasty', Hong Kong Museum of Art, 1978, no. 14. For a discussion of the significance of the *yuzhi* form of mark, see no. 1 above.

1. Hong Kong Museum. 'Snuff Bottles of the Ch'ing Dynasty', *Catalogue*, no. 15, October 1978.

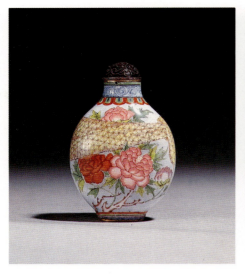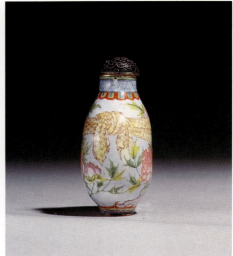

9

Painted enamels on copper; polychrome; with a continuous design of peonies enclosed by a diaper brocade around the shoulders, knotted on one side, the base inscribed in blue *Qianlong nianzhi (made in the Qianlong period); height: 4.8cm.*

Guangzhou Imperial ware; 1736-1795

    PROVENANCE: A.W. Bahr
                       R.H. Ellsworth
                       Sotheby's New York, 3rd October 1980, lot 173
                       Eric Young
                       Sotheby's London, 3rd March 1987, lot 66

Apart from Beijing, the other great centre for enamelling in China was Guangzhou. The enamelling workshops in Guangzhou probably started at about the same date as those in Beijing, circa 1710-1715, but a large part of their output was geared to export. Nevertheless, a significant number of items were sent from Guangzhou, throughout the eighteenth century as court tribute to Beijing, and numerous Palace presentation lists survive, in the archives of the Palace Museum in Beijing which list these tributes[1].

Amongst these documented items are numerous enamelled snuff bottles and a close study reveals many stylistic differences with the enamelled wares of Beijing. The actual painting techniques of Guangzhou involved extensive use of line and wash as is clearly seen in this example and in number 11 below. The enamels of Beijing, particularly when small items such as snuff bottles, boxes or panels are involved, are almost invariably painted in a minutely stippled technique similar to that employed in European enamelling.

This technique would have been taught to the craftsmen of Beijing by the Jesuits skilled in these arts based at Court.

In addition, the wares of Guangzhou are, in general significantly less finely painted artistically, though frequently technically as fine. This particular example is one of the best Guangzhou bottles recorded but it still betrays its origins in the slightly stiff outlines of the peony branches.

Finally, an examination of the way in which the reign marks are written is instructive. The Beijing reign marks, although written by several different hands, invariably employ thick brush-strokes with a tendency to place a line rather than a dot, in the centre of the box forming part of the left hand component of the character *qian*, whereas the Guangzhou brush-strokes tend to be thinner, with a dot rather than a line in the box forming part of the left hand of the *qian* character.

1. Yang Boda. *Tributes from Guangdong to the Qing Court.*

10

Painted enamels on copper; polychrome; with a panel on front enclosing a European lady and on the reverse a bearded gentleman, the shoulders with feathery grisaille scrolls; *height: 5.4cm*.

Guangzhou; 1710-1730

PROVENANCE: Sotheby's, New York, 3rd November 1982, lot 238
Hugh Moss
The Belfort Collection

EXHIBITED: Hong Kong Museum of Art, October 1978

PUBLISHED: *Journal* of the I.C.S.B.S., December 1977, p. 31, nos 67/8
Hong Kong Museum. *Catalogue*, no. 94

A very early example of Guangzhou enamel. The feathery pencilled grisaille scrolls on the shoulders are typical of decoration on a variety of wares from the late Kangxi period and the relative crudeness of the two figures postulates an early date before techniques became more refined. The simple diaper pattern on the neck is identical to that on the rim of a pair of dishes exhibited at the Ashmolean Museum, Oxford, dated to the late Kangxi period[1].

All these early Guangzhou wares appear to have an unusually heavy metal body, a trait which is possessed by this bottle, as well.

1. M. Gillingham. *Chinese Painted Enamels*, 1978, p. 12, no. 2.

11

Painted enamels on copper; polychrome; with European figures and a dog in a landscape, a turreted building in the background, an archaistic interlaced scroll around the shoulders, the base inscribed in blue *Qianlong nianzhi (made in the Qianlong period); height: 7.2cm.*

Guangzhou; 1736-1795

A classic example of the Guangzhou style with the broad wash strokes in the clothing of the figures. The artist has had some difficulty with the European faces and a comparison with the treatment of European faces in Beijing reveals a significant difference. The various borders, especially the dotted band around the base, the yellow angular scroll on the shoulders and the line borders around the neck are typical of Guangzhou, as is the rather elongated oval shape, which is not found in Beijing. The reign mark has similar characteristics to that of number 9 above.

Enamels on Glass

Painted enamels on glass; white glass with polychrome enamels; the front painted with a lady elaborately dressed, holding a fish, the reverse with a similarly dressed lady, a basket tucked over one arm, each of the sides with puce panels depicting European-style buildings, a minutely pencilled classic scroll on the shoulders beneath acanthus leaves, the base with an incised mark *Qianlong nianzhi (made in the Qianlong period)*, filled in with blue enamels; *height: 6.2cm.*

Beijing Palace Workshops; 1736-1795

      PROVENANCE: S.L. Levine, Sotheby's New York, 11th October 1979, lot 33
                           The Belfort Collection

      PUBLISHED: V. Jutheau. *Tabatières Chinoises*, cover and p.p. 78 and 79

An almost identical bottle is in the National Palace Museum, Taiwan[1]. Whilst the same hand is almost certainly responsible for both these bottles, together with a glass brushpot in the Percival David Foundation and another brushpot illustrated by Moss[2], it is of interest to note that the two bottles depict Chinese figures in European dress whereas the other vessels depict European figures[6]. In the very European aspect of the faces of the figures on the bottles it is tempting to see a European hand at work. The puce panels on the sides are probably copied from contemporary European enamel samples sent to the Court.

The enamelled glass wares represent a combination of the output of two of the ateliers in the Palace Workshops. A glass making workshop provided the bodies for the enamelling workshop, with the typical wheel-cut mark on the base.

The art of enamelling on glass posed far greater technical problems than that of enamelling on porcelain or copper. High alkaline glass has a low fusion point and if this point is reached before the maturation of the enamels, the vessel will collapse[3]. White glass contained tin oxide which would have helped to stabilise the body.

Only one enamelled glass vessel attributed to the Kangxi period and a single enamelled glass snuff bottle from the Yongzheng period have been recorded[4], demonstrating the difficulties which must have been faced by the early workers in this field. The Qianlong Emperor, however, clearly persisted in the pursuit of this art and to a large extent was successful. Forty three enamelled glass bottles, each of a different design, survive in the National Palace Museum, Taiwan[5], and a small number exists in Museums and private collections in the West.

The reign mark of this and the following two examples has been wheel-cut in the usual way and then filled in with blue enamels in an effort, largely successful, to render the mark neater.

1. *Masterpieces of Chinese Snuff Bottles in the National Palace Museum, Taiwan*, p. 22.
2. H. Moss. *By Imperial Command*, p. 35.
3. H. Moss. *op cit*, p. 59.
4. H. Moss. *op cit*, Pl. 33/34.
5. Lin-sheng Chang. *Journal* of the I.C.S.B.S., March 1979.
6. A dish in the National Palace Museum, Taiwan with a very similar Chinese figure is illustrated in the *Catalogue of Ch'ing Porcelain, Ch'ien Lung Ware*, pl. 70.

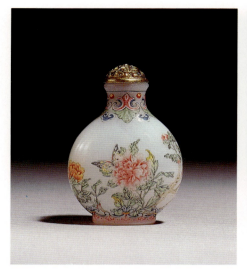
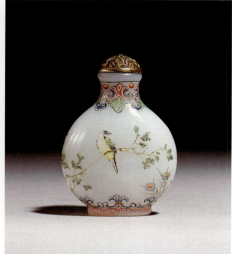

13

Painted enamels on glass; white glass with polychrome enamels; the front with leafy clusters of peonies, a branch extending around the reverse with a yellow-throated bird perched on it, the collar with pomegranate motifs and acanthus leaves, interspersed by small *ruyi* heads, the foot encircled by a band of interlaced trefoil motifs, the base incised *Qianlong nianzhi (made in the Qianlong period)* and filled in with blue enamels; *height: 4.5cm.*

Beijing Palace Workshops; 1736-1795

PROVENANCE: Arthur Gadsby
A Scottish Private Collection
Hugh Moss

PUBLISHED: H. Moss. *By Imperial Command*, pl. 39

The slightly opalescent body of this bottle allows the light to shine faintly through, imparting a luminosity to the decoration. This is a characteristic feature of enamelled glass.

A bottle which is stylistically very similar to this one is in the Seattle Art Museum, Washington, U.S.A.[1] Both examples compare very closely with imperial porcelain wares in the treatment of the leaves and petals on the flowers. The incised mark on this bottle has been rendered neater with the use of blue enamels, and is flush with the surface, a characteristic which is not evident in the group of later copies which will be discussed below.

1. Hong Kong Museum. 'Snuff Bottles of the Ch'ing Dynasty', *Catalogue*, no. 21, October 1978.

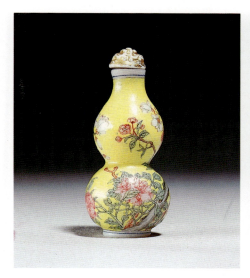
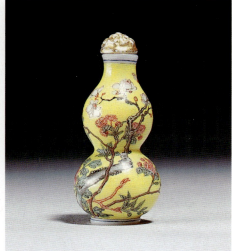

14
___

Painted enamels on glass; white glass with polychrome enamels; of double-gourd shape painted with a scene of flowering magnolia, the trunk extending around the whole body, with peonies at the foot, all reserved on a yellow enamel ground, the base incised *Qianlong nianzhi (made in the Qianlong period)*, and filled in with blue enamels; *height: 5.5cm*.

Beijing Palace Workshops; 1736-1795

PROVENANCE:	Barbara Hutton
	Sotheby's London, 6th July 1971, lot 163
	Hugh Moss
	The Belfort Collection
EXHIBITED:	Hong Kong Museum of Art, October 1978
PUBLISHED:	Honolulu Museum. *Chinese Porcelain, The Barbara Hutton Collection*, p. 9
	V. Jutheau. *Tabatières Chinoises*, p. 76, fig. 6
	Hong Kong Museum of Art. *Catalogue*, no. 26

The yellow ground of this bottle is slightly uneven in colour, demonstrating that even by the reign of the Qianlong Emperor all technical problems in the control of the firing had not been overcome. Nevertheless, the quality of the painting is of the finest. The artist demonstrates complete control of the difficult form of the double-gourd in the natural way in which the decoration occupies the space available. Later copyists invariably let themselves down by failing to fill satisfactorily the space available (see no. 21 below).

An almost identical bottle, but decorated with bamboo and prunus is in the Collection of Mr. and Mrs. James Li, and another is in the Collection of Edward Choate O'Dell, *Catalogue*, no. 100[1].

1. John G. Ford. *Chinese Snuff Bottles. The Edward Choate O'Dell Collection.*

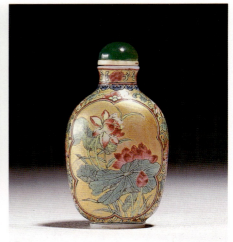

15

Painted enamels on glass; white glass with polychrome enamels on a gold ground; decorated on each side with a leaf-shaped panel enclosing a slightly differing cluster of flowering lotus, the shoulders with a stylised flowering scroll with broad leaves, all reserved on a gold enamel ground, the base incised *Qianlong nianzhi (made in the Qianlong period)* in seal characters filled in with orange enamels; *height: 5.3 cm.*

Beijing Palace Workshops; 1736-1795

PROVENANCE: A.W. Bahr
                    Hugh Moss
                    A Scottish Private Collection

PUBLISHED: A.W. Bahr. *Old Chinese Porcelain and Works of Art in China* (1911),
                    p. 143, pl. CII
                    H. Moss. *By Imperial Command*, pl. 40

No other Palace enamelled glass bottle of this shape appears to have been recorded. Nevertheless, the quality of the painting, particularly in the control exercised over the veining of the lotus leaves, is such that a palace origin cannot be doubted. In addition, the leaves of the flowering scroll have veining painted in lines which compares very closely with that to be found on many of the Palace enamelled bowls.[1] Finally the thin consistency of the gold ground compares to that found on many of the snuff bottles in the National Palace Museum, Taiwan.[2]

The reign mark on this bottle is worthy of note. It has been incised in seal script rather than the usual character script and is therefore of the utmost importance in helping to establish the Palace origin of the glass and jade bottles (nos. 24, 62, 64 and 65) in this exhibition. There are two bottles with identical incised seal marks in the National Palace Museum, Taiwan[3].

1.   See *Catalogue* of Ch'ing Porcelain, Chien Lung Ware in the National Palace Museum, Republic of China, pls. 57-61.
2&3. Lin-sheng Chang. *Journal* of the I.C.S.B.S., March 1979.

16

Painted enamels on glass; clear glass with polychrome enamels; a continuous scene depicting prunus in blossom, bamboo and a peony springing from rockwork, the base inscribed in red *guyuexuan (old moon pavilion)*; *height: 6.1cm.*

Beijing; 1770-1795

PROVENANCE: Sotheby's New York, 3rd October 1980, lot 80
                      Dr. Paula Hallett
                      Sotheby's, 27th June 1986, lot 33

Much has been written about the meaning of the term *guyuexuan*[1], both in China and in the West. The term has come to be applied, quite wrongly, to the group of palace-enamelled snuff bottles, porcelains and other wares, discussed above, whereas it should properly be applied only to the small group of snuff bottles, vases and other wares which either bear a *guyuexuan* mark or are stylistically similar to this bottle with Qianlong marks, or no marks at all.

The use of hall marks on the base of wares was common in China, and Moss suggests[2] that the *guyuexuan* mark was added to the products of a private kiln in Beijing working between 1770 and 1850 to supply small wares to the nobility.

The thinness of the enamels and the stylistic simplicity of this particular bottle, which compares closely to the type of decoration to be found on Qianlong-marked wares particularly vases and bowls, suggest a date of manufacture late in the Qianlong reign.

1. S. Yorke Hardy. 'Ku Yueh-Hsuän: a New Hypothesis', *Oriental Art*, Vol II, No. 3, Winter 1949-1950.
2. H. Moss. 'Enamelled glass wares of the Ku Yueh-Hsuän Group,' *Journal* of the I.C.S.B.S., June 1978.

17

17

Painted enamels on glass; clear glass with polychrome enamels; delicately painted with a continuous scene depicting asters, bamboo and peach blossom springing from an ornamental rock, a frieze of detached flowering sprigs around the neck; *height: 4.3 cm.*

Beijing; 1770-1795

PROVENANCE: Robert Hall

Although there is no mark on the base of this bottle, it clearly belongs to the same group as number 16. The style of painting, the thinness of the enamels and the general colour tones are almost identical.

18

Painted enamels on glass; white glass carved in relief with polychrome enamels; decorated with a continuous scene of two coiled *chilong* each biting at sprays of *lingzhi* fungus, the base inscribed in red *guyuexuan (ancient moon pavilion); height: 5.5 cm.*

Beijing; 1800-1850

PROVENANCE: Sotheby's New York, 27th June 1986, lot 67

A small group of enamelled snuff bottles with carved decoration exists. Most of these[1] bear the *guyuexuan* mark on the base, and the style of their decoration and the tone of the enamels suggest that they are a later development of the same kiln in Beijing which was responsible for nos. 16 and 17 above.

It is very rare to find the subject-matter depicted on this particular bottle. The majority of this group depicts birds or clusters of flowers.

1. H. Moss. *Chinese Snuff Bottles*, No. 6.

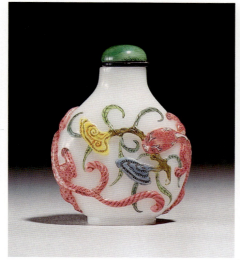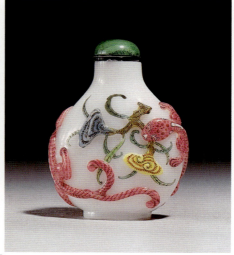

18

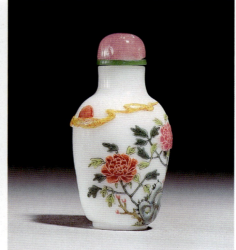

19

19

Painted enamels on glass; carved glass with polychrome enamels; decorated with a continuous scene depicting a phoenix perched on an ornamental rock, surrounded by clusters of flowers, the sun setting behind billowing clouds, the base inscribed in red *guyuexuan (ancient moon pavilion); height: 5.7cm.*

Beijing; 1800-1850

PROVENANCE: Robert Hall

The phoenix [*fenghuang*] is one of the most popular images in Chinese art. It is the second of the four miraculous creatures, the dragon being the first, the unicorn the third and the tortoise the fourth.

The phoenix is the ruler of all those which are feathered and is the symbol of the female.

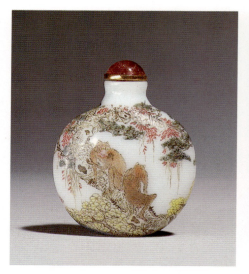
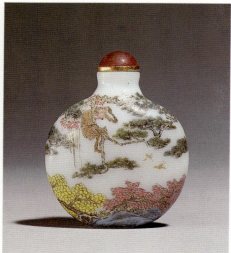

20

Painted enamels on glass; white glass with polychrome enamels; with a continuous scene of monkeys climbing amongst flowering wisteria, other bushes in blossom around the foot, a sylised archaistic dragon in yellow on the base; *height: 5.5cm.*

Guangzhou; 1770-1850

    PROVENANCE: Hugh Moss

This bottle forms part of a distinctive group, many of which have neatly written Qianlong seal marks on the base. However, the dragon on the base of this example provides an important clue as to its origins, as this type of dragon is often found on Guangzhou enamel wares on copper.

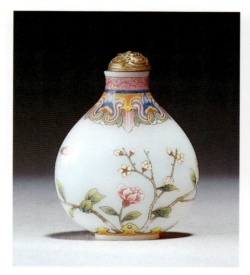
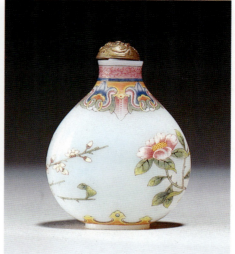

21

Painted enamels on glass; white glass with polychrome enamels; decorated with a continuous design of flowering mallow and peach blossom, an elaborate collar on the neck and a trefoil border around the foot, the base inscribed in blue, *Qianlong nianzhi (made in the Qianlong period)*; *height: 5.7 cm.*

Ye Family Workshops, Beijing, by Ye Bengqi; circa 1930-1945

PROVENANCE: J.T. Wakefield
Sotheby's London, 6th May 1986, lot 287

This bottle represents the last of the four distinctive groups of enamelled glass wares. It was made by Ye Bengqi, a member of a family of four, best known for their skills at painting inside snuff bottles. Moss interviewed Bengqi in Beijing in 1974 and obtained first-hand evidence of the activities of the family[1].

They used to visit the Beijing Museum and memorise the patterns depicted on the authentic enamelled glass bottles and wares on display. They would then attempt to recreate them.

There is no doubt as to the technical mastery achieved by the Ye. There is almost none of the pitting to be found on the eighteenth century examples and the enamels have a uniform brilliance. However a comparison of the style of painting and the colour tones of the enamels soon reveals differences[2]. The originals are painted with freedom and vigour, the actual brush-strokes providing the form of the petals, tree-trunks and other details, whereas the designs on the Ye bottles are all first outlined and then filled in. The enamels themselves are much thicker and more opaque than those of the earlier examples and there exists, quite commonly, a rich ochre colour, usually found on rocks, collars and base decoration which cannot be found on the originals. Finally, the enamelled marks on the base are invariably painted in raised enamel standing on the surface. The marks of the originals were incised in the glass workshops and filled in with blue enamels so that they rested flush with the surface. This was not a detail which would have been apparent to the Ye, pearing through the glass of the vitrines in the museum at the genuine articles.

1. H. Moss. 'The Apricot Grove Studio, Part III,' *Journal* of the I.C.S.B.S., Autumn 1985.
2. See number 13 above.

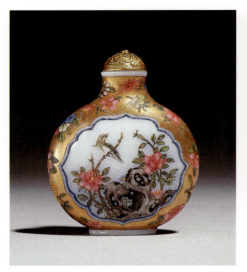

22

Painted enamels on glass; white glass with polychrome enamels; painted on each side with a barbed quatrefoil panel enclosing a bird perched on a branch of tree peony and a butterfly hovering above peach blossom, reserved on a gold ground scattered with numerous different flowering sprigs, the base inscribed in blue *Qianlong nianzhi (made in the Qianlong period)*; *height: 5.7cm.*

Ye Family Workshops, Beijing, by Ye Bengqi; circa 1930-1945

PROVENANCE: Gerd Lester

A rare example of a gold-ground bottle from these workshops. It is still not possible to identify exactly which bottles were painted by Ye Bengqi and which were merely products of the workshops, but this bottle is a good candidate for Bengqi himself. The bird perched on the branch compares very closely to the birds painted by Bengqi on his inside-painted bottles[1], and the white background to this bottle has been delicately stippled in blue to provide added depth, a sophisticated technique one might expect from the master of the school.

Ye Bengqi died in 1975 but he in turn taught the leading inside-painted artist of the modern era, Wang Xisan, the art of enamelling on glass, so the skill has been preserved[2].

1. Lilla Perry. *Chinese Snuff Bottles*, p. 135, fig. 131.
2. H. Moss. *By Imperial Command*, p. 49.

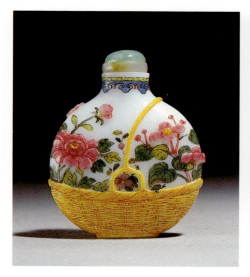
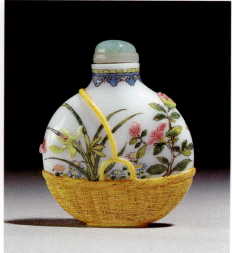

23

Painted enamels on glass; white glass carved in relief with polychrome enamels; in the form of a basket-full of flowers, including narcissus, mallow and peony, a *ruyi*-head band around the neck, the base inscribed in blue *yuzhi (by imperial command)*; *height: 5.8cm.*

Ye Family Workshops, Beijing, by Ye Bengqi; circa 1930-1945

PROVENANCE: Lilla S. Perry
                    Bob C. Stevens
                    The Belfort Collection

EXHIBITED: Hong Kong Museum of Art, October 1978

PUBLISHED: Bob C. Stevens. *The Collector's Book of Snuff Bottles*, no. 957
                    Hong Kong Museum. *Catalogue*, no. 29
                    H.M. Moss. *Journal* of the I.C.S.B.S., June 1978, p. 13, fig. 4
                    Journal of the I.C.S.B.S., December 1978, p. 36, fig. 29

For many years this bottle was believed to belong to the group of carved and enamelled wares discussed above[1]. However an examination of the enamels themselves reveals a close affinity with the enamels to be found on the other bottles of the Ye group.

The clue lies in the colour tones of the blue collar around the neck and the green of the leaves. Each of these compares almost exactly with its counterpart on no. 22 above, and yet they cannot be found on the earlier group.

An example of this subject from the earlier group is in the Exeter Collection[2] at Burghley House, and the enamels are both less bright and considerably thinner. Finally, the mark, *yuzbi*, purports to be very important. Whilst earlier bottles often had wrongly inscribed Qianlong marks, the hierarchy of marks and the importance of the *yuzbi* mark was not generally understood outside the ambit of the Palace. By the early twentieth century, with the break-down of the Qing establishment at Court, imperially marked objects began to find their way onto the market and the imitations began.

1. See numbers 18 and 19.
2. H. Moss. *Chinese Snuff Bottles*, No. 6, p. 105, E.7.

Jade

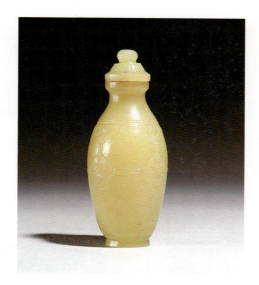

24

Nephrite; of yellow tone, the ovoid body carved in low relief overall with interlaced ropework joining numerous cash, suspended from a *ruyi*-head border, the base with an incised seal mark *Qianlong nianzhi* (*made in the Qianlong period*), matching stopper; *height: 6.3cm.*

Beijing Palace Workshops; 1736-1795

    PROVENANCE: Christies New York, 9th May 1981, lot 399
                       Hugh Moss
                       The Belfort Collection

Jade has occupied a unique place of importance in China for several thousand years. It is valued far above gold or precious stones and has connotations of symbolism and mystique found in no other material. 'How much are the ancients to be envied. They had among them men of such wisdom as to know that nothing else is worthy of being mentioned on the same day as jade.'[1]

The term 'jade' covers two distinct minerals, nephrite and jadeite. Nephrite is a silicate containing calcium, magnesium and aluminium and has a hardness of 6.5 on the Moh's Scale. It tends to be an opaque creamy material, most prized in pure white or yellow, but found in numerous other colours ranging from pale grey through various shades of green to black.

Jadeite, on the other hand, is a silicate of sodium and aluminium. As a material it tends towards translucency with an 'icy' structure apparent to the naked eye. Although jadeite also exists in a full range of colours, it is most highly prized when it is of flawless emerald-green tone.[2]

The Qianlong Emperor was, perhaps, the greatest patron of jades in Chinese history. Enormous quantities of jade objects were made throughout the major jade carving regions of China and sent to the Palace as tribute. The bulk of these did not have reign marks or other identifying marks.

The Palace Workshops were involved in the manufacture of small jade objects, mainly for the scholars table, and many of these possess either reign marks or inscriptions of Imperial poems[3]. The reign marks are unusually neatly incised with four characters in seal script as in this example.

This bottle is beautifully crafted, particularly in the low relief carving which is crisply executed and the surface polishing, which is as smooth as possible. The ropework pattern was one favoured by the Palace Workshops and can be found on numerous items (see number 4 above).

The warm yellowish tone of the material, known as the colour of steamed chestnuts, is very rare and prized and is caused by iron impurities.

1. Quoted by Tsang and Moss. *Arts from the Scholar's Studio*, no. 179.
2. For a discussion of the sources of jade available to the Chinese, see Rawson & Ayers, *Chinese Jade Throughout the Ages*, O.C.S. London 1975.
3. Yang Boda and Wango Weng. *The Palace Museum, Peking*, pp. 264/5.

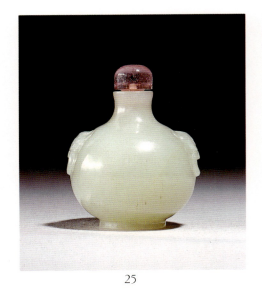

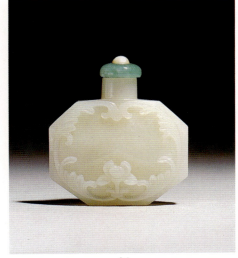

25   26

25

Nephrite; of white colour and rounded section, with mask and ring handles on the shoulders, the base incised with the seal mark *Qianlong nianzhi* (*made in the Qianlong period*); *height: 4.3cm.*

Beijing Palace Workshops; 1736-1795

    PROVENANCE: Hugh Moss
                      Emily Byrne Curtis

The seal mark on this bottle is identical with that of the preceding bottle. It is of the small size generally found on snuff bottles of all types attributable to the Palace Workshops.

26

Nephrite; of flattened form, faceted on each side and carved in relief with a border of stylised Indian lotus scrolls; *height: 4.8cm.*

Attributed to the Beijing Palace Workshops; Qianlong period, 1736-1795

    PROVENANCE: The Ko Collection
                      Christies London
                      Bob C. Stevens
                      Sotheby's Honolulu, November 7th 1981, lot 115
                      Alice B. McReynolds
                      Sotheby's Los Angeles, October 31st, 1984, lot 158

    EXHIBITED: Hong Kong Museum of Art, October 1977, *Catalogue* of Chinese Snuff Bottles, no. 136
                      Mikimoto Hall, Tokyo, October 1978, *Catalogue* of the Stevens Collection, no. 164

    PUBLISHED: *Journal* of the I.C.S.B.S., June 1978, p. 45 and Dec. 1978, p. 43

The faceted form was popular in the Palace and is found on numerous marked examples in glass.[1] It is rare to find this shape in jade, but the quality of the carving and the treatment of the subject matter are both suggestive of a Palace Workshop origin.

1. See numbers 69-71 below.

27

28

27

Nephrite; carved on each side in graduated relief with a central medallion of crossed keys enclosed by a border of shell-like motifs, mask and ring handles on the shoulders; *height: 5.2cm.*

Attributed to the Beijing Palace Workshops; Qianlong period, 1736-1795

    PROVENANCE: Gerd Lester

    PUBLISHED: E. B. Curtis. *Arts of Asia*, January-February 1982, p. 89

This bottle exhibits considerable European influence in the motifs of its design. The crossed keys of St. Peter adorn the centre and the baroque shell-like border is reminiscent of the shell-motifs which decorated the *yuan, ming-yuan*, the Summer Palace, built for the Qianlong Emperor under Jesuit supervision[1]. Such a sophisticated combination of foreign motifs would be more likely to have originated from the Palace Workshops than from one of the Provincial centres and the subtly graduated relief carving is of the highest quality.

1. Wan Yi. *Life in the Forbidden City*, p. 277.

28

Nephrite; carved overall with a pattern of overlapping lotus petals with details incised, the base formed from further petals; *height: 5.2cm.*

Attributed to the Beijing Palace Workshops; Qianlong period, 1736-1795

    PROVENANCE: Gerd Lester

The rounded and subtle quality of the carving on this bottle relate well to the preceding two examples. Once again the quality of the nephrite is flawless and of the pure white variety most prized by the Chinese at this period.

The lotus is of the utmost importance in Chinese folklore and symbolism, due in part to Buddhist influence. It is one of the eight Buddhist 'Precious objects' and a symbol of enlightenment as it grows out of the muddy depths to flower in the light above. The lotus is also regarded as the emblem of Summer and fruitfulness.

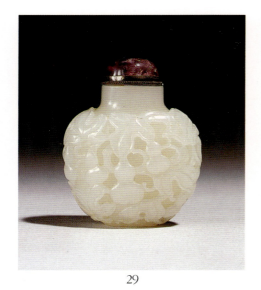

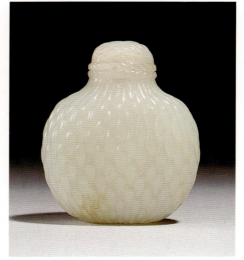

29   30

29

Nephrite; carved in deep relief with an overall pattern of fruiting double-gourds enveloped by leafy fronds; *height: 5.2cm.*

18th Century

    PROVENANCE: Sotheby's London, 2nd May 1985, lot 485

It is difficult to draw the line between items actually manufactured within the Palace Workshops and items manufactured at other centres to be sent to the Palace. In many respects the place of manufacture is not, in itself, important provided the quality of the piece is of the highest.

In this example, the quality of polishing and the overall integrity and vigour of the design leave one in no doubt as to its Qianlong period origins.

The double-gourd, which grows naturally in this form, is a miniature replica of heaven and earth; in its shape it unites the two. An object decorated with double-gourd scrolls expresses the wish for 'Ten thousand generations of sons and grandsons'.

30

Nephrite: carved overall with a 'wickerwork' pattern bordered by a rope on the mouth, repeated on the matching stopper; *height: 5.2cm.*

18th Century

    PROVENANCE: Christies, London, 14th June 1985, lot 110
                    Dr. Paula Hallett

This bottle has an unusually wide opening to the mouth, extending the full diameter of the neck. It is rare to find a stopper carved to match the bottle.

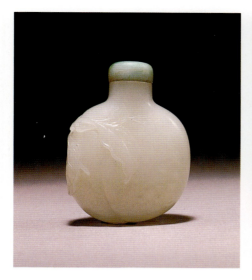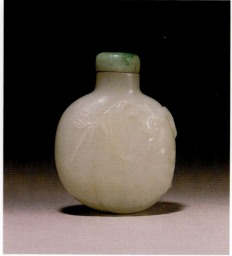

31

Nephrite; carved in the form of a fruiting pomegranate, the seeds showing on one side, the shoulders enveloped by broad leaves extending from a gnarled stalk; *height: 4.8cm*.

18th Century

     PROVENANCE: J.T. Wakefield
                        Sotheby's London, 6th May 1986, lot 240

The low relief carving and incised details on this bottle are both typical of eighteenth century Chinese carving and are elements which can be found on numerous artifacts of this period.

A ripe pomegranate with seeds spilling out of its sides is a popular wedding present as it expresses the wish *liu kai baizi* (the pomegranate opens: one hundred seeds, one hundred sons). The word *zi* in Chinese can mean both 'seed' and 'son'.

The pomegranate, which flowers in the fifth Chinese month, is one of the blossoms of the four seasons, together with the orchid, the iris and the wild apple.

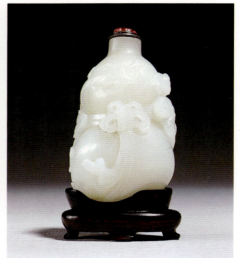

32

Nephrite; of double-gourd form with a knotted sash around the centre, a clump of *lingzhi* fungus on one shoulder and leaves trailing tendrils opposite, the base finished as a hole for the stalk; *height: 6.7cm*.

18th Century

    PROVENANCE: Hugh Moss
                        C.S. Wilkinson
                        Cyril Green
                        The Belfort Collection

    EXHIBITED: Hong Kong Museum of Art, October 1978
                        Arcade Chaumet, Paris, June 1982, *Catalogue*, no. 195

    PUBLISHED: H. Moss. *Chinese Snuff Bottles*, No. 2, p. 27, fig. 1
                        Hong Kong Museum. *Catalogue*, no. 161
                        V. Jutheau. *Tabatières Chinoises*, p. 112, fig. 4

The *lingzhi* is a fungus reputed to grant Immortality. It is also a symbol of all that is bright and good, and is one of the most commonly depicted of all Chinese art motifs.

Nephrite; of spinach colour, supported on a neatly finished footrim, the base incised *Xingyouheng tang (The Hall of Constancy)*; *height: 5.5cm*; together with a matching dish.

1810-1854

    PROVENANCE: Hugh Moss

    EXHIBITED: Hong Kong Museum of Art, October 1978

    PUBLISHED: Hong Kong Museum. *Catalogue*, no. 176

Xingyouheng Tang belonged to the fifth Prince Ding, Zaichuan, a great-great-grandson of the Qianlong Emperor[1]. He is known to have collected a range of scholarly articles, paintings and snuff bottles between 1810 and 1854. This particular bottle, which is very well hollowed out and perfectly finished, is typical of the type he favoured.

1. See number 141 below for a detailed review of this figure.

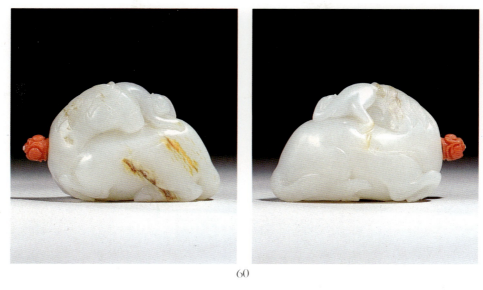

60

61

61

Nephrite; of pure white tone carved as twin fish, each linked together by water-plants across the base to form a double bottle, *length: 7.5cm*.

Qianlong period, 1736-1795

    PROVENANCE: Hugh Moss

A bottle which might be mistaken for a pendant conversion. However, the large size and the depth of the carving would make it unsuitable for such use and the finish of the fishes' mouths is such that they were clearly made to surround a hollow area and receive stoppers.

Glass

62

Glass; of flattened form, the clear metal suffused with crizzling and dappled overall with blue splashes, the base incised with the seal mark *Qianlong nianzbi (made in the Qianlong period)*; *height: 5.2cm.*

Beijing Palace Workshops; 1736-1795

PROVENANCE: Hugh Moss
                   The Belfort Collection

EXHIBITED: Hong Kong Museum of Art, October 1978
                Arcade Chaumet, Paris, June 1982, *Catalogue*, no. 77

PUBLISHED: Hong Kong Museum. *Catalogue*, no. 64

A workshop for the manufacture of glass was one of the first to be set up in the Palace, under the supervision of the Jesuit, Father Killian Stumpff, in the early 1680's. There is ample documentary evidence of the Kangxi Emperor's liking for glass and glass snuff bottles[1] with Wanghao recording the gift of a glass snuff bottle from the Emperor as early as 1703.

Whilst we have no evidence as to the appearance of these early glass bottles, it is likely that they were of simple form and undecorated, relying for their appeal on their multitude of colours.

This bottle, with its neatly incised seal mark, which compares closely with that found on the enamelled glass bottle, number 15 above, is undoubtedly of Palace origin. The crizzled effect in the glass is due to a slight decomposition in the surface due to an incorrect mix of materials at the time of manufacture. This fault was quite common in the earlier Palace glass wares.

1. See G. Tsang and H. Moss. Introduction to the *Catalogue*, 'Snuff Bottles of the Ch'ing Dynasty'. Hong Kong Museum of Art, October 1978.

62

63

63

Glass; of miniature size, supported on a neatly finished footrim, the black metal suffused with gold dappling, the base incised with the four character mark *Qianlong nianzhi* (*made in the Qianlong period*); *height: 2.8cm.*

Beijing Palace Workshops; 1736-1795

    PROVENANCE: Hugh Moss
                         The Belfort Collection

    EXHIBITED: Hong Kong Museum of Art, October 1978
                         Arcade Chaumet, Paris, June 1982, *Catalogue*, no. 83

    PUBLISHED: Hong Kong Museum. *Catalogue*, no. 85

The rather crude wheel-cut four character mark on the base of this bottle is more common than the very finely incised seal mark of number 62 above. This type of mark appears to have been common in the Palace Workshops[1] and it appears on several bottles in the Palace Museum, Taiwan. The enamelled glass bottles in this exhibition which posses a wheel-cut four character mark have had those marks smartened up with blue enamels, although a few such palace enamel wares possess unfilled wheel-cut marks.

1. G. Tsang and H. Moss. *Arts from the Scholar's Studio*, no. 124.

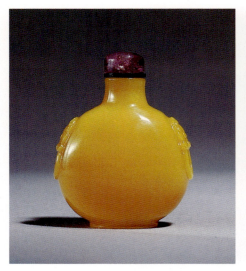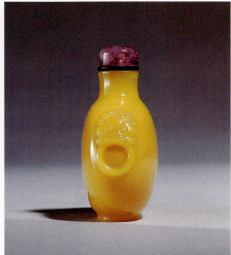

64

Glass; of rich imperial yellow tone supported on a neatly finished footrim, the shoulders carved with mask and ring handles, the base incised with the four character seal mark *Qianlong yuzhi* (*made by imperial order of Qianlong*); *height: 5.8cm.*

Beijing Palace Workshops; 1736-1795

   PROVENANCE: Gerd Lester

The seal mark on this bottle, neatly incised, denotes that there was a direct imperial interest in its manufacture. The hierarchy of marks in use in the Palace Workshops has already been explained (number 1 above). Yellow was a colour reserved during the Ming and Qing Dynasties solely for imperial use. There was no standard tone of yellow prescribed and imperial yellow objects exist in many different shades ranging from a bright lemon-yellow through to a rich egg-yolk yellow.

65

Glass; of imperial yellow tone supported on a neatly finished footrim, the shoulders with mask and ring handles, the base incised with the four character seal mark *Qianlong nianzhi* (*made in the Qianlong period*); *height: 6.1cm*.

Beijing Palace Workshops; 1736-1795

PROVENANCE: Hugh Moss
             The Belfort Collection

EXHIBITED: Hong Kong Museum of Art, October 1978
             Arcade Chaumet, Paris, June 1982 *Catalogue*, no. 67

PUBLISHED: Hong Kong Museum. *Catalogue*, No. 58
             V. Jutheau. *Tabatières Chinoises*, p. 58, figs. 3 and 4

The neatly incised seal mark on this bottle is almost identical with that on the base of the enamelled glass bottle number 15 above.[1]

The mask and ring handles on the shoulders are inspired by the *taotie* masks which are one of the most common decorative motifs to be found on ancient Chinese bronze wares. These masks are usually stylised bovine or dragon's heads.

1. Compare also the seal mark on the rock crystal water vessel, illustrated by Tsang and Moss, *Arts From the Scholar's Studio*, no. 93.

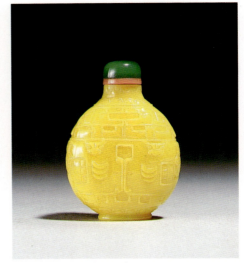

66   67

66

Glass; imperial yellow, carved around the centre with a frieze of confronted archaistic dragons, divided on the the shoulders by horned bovine masks, between bands of petal lappets and an incised brocade diaper; *height: 6.3cm.*

Attributed to the Beijing Palace Workshops; Qianlong period, 1736-1795

PROVENANCE:	Hugh Moss
	The Belfort Collection
EXHIBITED:	Hong Kong Museum of Art, October 1978
	Arcade Chaumet, Paris, June 1982 *Catalogue*, no. 69
PUBLISHED:	Hong Kong Museum. *Catalogue*, No. 65
	Journal of the I.C.S.B.S., December, 1975, p. 12, no. 53

An almost identical bottle, in the Collection of Edgar S. Wise of California, possesses the four character mark of *Qianlong*,[1] thereby allowing an attribution to the Palace Workshops for this bottle. The quality of the carving is of the highest, the treatment of the petal lappets being particularly noteworthy and the archaic bronze dragon motifs were a popular decorative device during the eighteenth century.

1. Illustrated by Bob C. Stevens. *The Collector's Book of Snuff Bottles*, no. 186.

67

Glass; imperial yellow, of small size carved on each side with a stylised *taotie* mask beneath a frieze of confronted archaic dragons, a band of petal lappets around the base, the shoulders with stylised pairs of archaic birds, beneath horned bovine heads; *height: 4.4cm.*

Attributed to the Beijing Palace Workshops; Qianlong period, 1736-1795

    PROVENANCE: Dr. Paula Hallett

The style and quality of carving on this bottle relate very closely to that of the previous example. The horned bovine heads on the shoulders of both are identical, and the paired birds are classic archaic bronze motifs.

68

69

68

Glass; imperial yellow, of baluster form supported on a neatly finished footrim, the shoulders carved with four mask and ring handles; *height: 5.8cm.*

Attributed to the Beijing Palace Workshops; Qianlong period, 1736-1795

The quality of carving on this bottle compares very closely with that of the preceding group, allowing an attribution to the Palace Workshops.

69

Glass; of small size with a raised faceted panel on each side, the material of pale lemon-yellow tone; *height: 3.7cm.*

Attributed to the Beijing Palace Workshops; Qianlong period, 1736-1795

PROVENANCE: Hugh Moss
                  The Belfort Collection

PUBLISHED: Hong Kong Museum. *Catalogue*, no. 59
                 V. Jutheau. *Tabatières Chinoises*, p. 60, fig. 4
                 Journal of the I.C.S.B.S., December 1975, p. 10, no. 39

This bottle is a classic example of the lemon-yellow tone which was particularly popular in the Yongzheng period. A glass vase from the Edward Chow Collection of this colour with a Yongzheng mark was sold by Sotheby's Hong Kong on 19th May, 1981, lot 608. (See the following bottle for comment on the faceted form.)

70   71

70

Glass; greenish-turquoise, of small size with a raised faceted panel on each side; *height: 3.5cm*.

Attributed to the Beijing Palace Workshops; Qianlong period, 1736-1795

    PROVENANCE: Hugh Moss
                        Dr. Paula Hallett

    PUBLISHED: V. Jutheau. *Tabatières Chinoises*, p. 63, fig. 1

A distinctive group of glass snuff bottle exists, all of which are of small size with faceted sides or panels. A few examples have been enamelled[1] and many of them bear the wheel-cut reign marks characteristic of the Palace Workshops[2]. Although this bottle bears no reign mark its similarity in size and finish to the marked examples allows an attribution to the Palace Workshops. There are traces of polishing on the base and it is possible that the reign mark was removed when the bottle found its way onto the market.

1. H. Moss. *By Imperial Command*, pl. 36.
2. H. Moss. 'An Imperial Habit', *Journal* of the I.C.S.B.S., Winter 1975, p. 3-15.

71

Glass; of small size and rich ruby-red tone, the shoulders faceted; *height; 3.8cm*.

Attributed to the Beijing Palace Workshops; Qianlong period, 1736-1795

The ruby-red tone of this bottle appears to have been particularly popular during the eighteenth century. The front and rear panels have been polished flat imparting a gem-like quality to the material when viewed from the side.

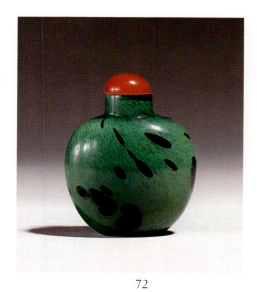

72   73

72

Glass; of spade shape with an applied layer of green dappled with black beneath an outer clear overlay; *height: 5.1cm.*

Attributed to Beijing; 18th Century

   PROVENANCE: Sotheby's London, 5th December, 1983, lot 19

This bottle forms part of a further distinctive group. Each is blown into a mould of similar shape and the decoration is then applied using various metallic oxides to impart the different colours. This layer is then covered by a clear glass overlay layer to protect and fix the decoration. The method of manufacture can be clearly seen when looking at the mouth rim where the differing layers become apparent.

The variety in colours presented by these bottles is enormous and no two appear to be the same. Their similarity to other glass wares of the eighteenth century, such as vases and small waterpots, together with their general patination points to this period as a date of manufacture. Beijing was not the only centre for the manufacture of glass and in the absence of identifying marks or styles, any attributions to Beijing as the place of manufacture must be tentative.

73

Glass; decorated with a layer of brilliant dark blue dappled with black splashes beneath a clear overlay; *height: 5.7cm.*

Attributed to Beijing; 18th Century

   PROVENANCE: Gerd Lester

74

75

74

Glass; of flattened form, the opalescent ground with scattered red splashes; *height: 4.8cm.*

Attributed to Beijing; 18th Century

    PROVENANCE: The Belfort Collection

    EXHIBITED: Arcade Chaumet, Paris, June 1982, *Catalogue*, no. 71

The opalescent hue to the body of this bottle is an effect often found in early Chinese glass. Whilst this bottle and the following group, (numbers 75-81) are all unmarked, they each have similarities with known marked examples which allows an attribution to Beijing[1].

1. See Hong Kong Museum of Art, October 1978, *Catalogue*, nos. 47, 56, 61, 67, 69 and 70.

75

Glass; of rich purple tone supported on a neatly finished footrim and with a flared mouth; *height: 4.3cm.*

Attributed to Beijing; 18th Century

    PROVENANCE: Dr. Paula Hallett
                        Sotheby's New York, 27th June, 1986, lot 30

A fine example of a beautifully finished bottle. Together with the elegance of its form, this combines to create a pleasing work of art from a very simple material. The rich colour is probably imitating amethyst.

76

Glass; of large size, the opalescent imperial yellow glass carved to depict an elephant with its legs forming the base, its head turned back and the *howdah* cloth incised with a diaper pattern, a *ruyi* head collar around the neck; *height: 7.6cm.*

Attributed to Beijing; Qianlong period, 1736-1795

It is rare to find a snuff bottle in the form of an elephant. The quality of carving and incised detail on this bottle compare closely with that found on jades dating from the Qianlong reign.

76

77

78

77

Glass; of flattened disc shape with a slightly concave base, one side with a pierced lug attached to the shoulders, the material of opalescent whitish tone; *height: 4.7cm.*

Attributed to Beijing; 18th Century

As the Chinese acquired mastery of the craft of glass-making they began to imitate different materials as in this example where nephrite is the source of the inspiration. It is unusual to find an attachment lug on a Snuff Bottle. As a general rule bottles were carried in small cloth bags suspended from the waist.

78

Glass; of ovoid form with swirling patterns of red beneath a clear overlay; *height: 5.7cm.*

Attributed to Beijing; 18th Century

   PROVENANCE: Gerd Lester

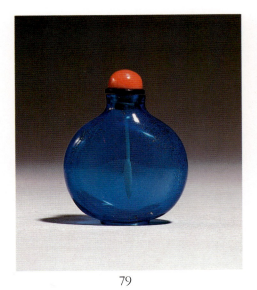

79   80

79

Glass; of small size and transparent blue tone, supported on a neatly finished footrim; *height:4.6cm*.

Attributed to Beijing; 18th Century

    PROVENANCE: Gerd Lester

This bottle exhibits crizzling on the interior similiar to number 62 above.

80

Glass; colourless, of small size with stepped shoulders and a splayed base; *height: 4.3cm*.

Attributed to Beijing; 1736-1795

    PROVENANCE: The Belfort Collection

    EXHIBITED: Arcade Chaumet, Paris, June 1982, *Catalogue*, no. 58

    PUBLISHED: V. Jutheau. *Tabatières Chinoises*, p. 59, fig. 1

A bottle of identical size and form, but with enamelled decoration similar in style to that of the *guyuexuan* group discussed above (numbers 16 and 17), is in the Collection of Mr. and Mrs. James Li[1] and it is possible that this bottle was a blank intended for similar enamelling.

1. H. Moss. 'Enamelled Glass Ware of the Ku Yueh Hsuan Group', *Journal* of the I.C.S.B.S., June 1978, p. 23, fig 36.

81

Glass; of opalescent turquoise-blue tone with faceted shoulders; *height: 5.5cm*.

Attributed to Beijing; 1820-1850

    PROVENANCE: Gerd Lester

This larger size of faceted bottle appears to have been favoured in the nineteenth century.

81

82

82

Glass; of turquoise colour with a raised faceted panel on each side decorated in gilding with a differing landscape scene, the shoulders decorated with a lotus scroll, the base incised and gilded with the four character mark *Daoguang nianzhi* (*made in the Daoguang period*); *height: 5.6cm.*

Beijing Palace Workshops; 1821-1850

    PROVENANCE: Gerd Lester

The Beijing Palace Workshops enjoyed their greatest output both in terms of quality and of quantity during the eighteenth century. None of the nineteenth century emperors devoted remotely as much attention or patronage to the workshops as their predecessors and consequently production declined.

This bottle is a survivor in style of the series of faceted bottles illustrated above. The gilded decoration is a device often used by the Chinese to enhance their monochrome porcelains, but it is not often found on snuff bottles.

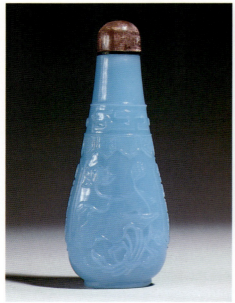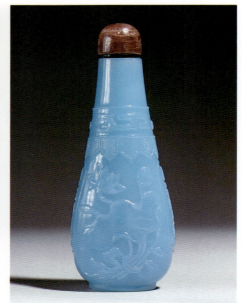

83

83

Glass; of turquoise colour carved on each side with a cluster of lotus beneath a collar of pendent stiff leaves and a frieze of archaistic dragons, each of the shoulders with a panel enclosing an inscription, the base incised *Guangxu nianzhi* (*made in the Guangxu period*); *height: 8.7cm.*

Attributed to the Beijing Palace Workshops; Guangxu period, 1874-1909

> PROVENANCE: Dr. Paula Hallett
> Sotheby's New York, 2nd December, 1985, lot 43

This bottle is similar in style, although carved in a stiffer manner, to the series of carved bottles illustrated above (numbers 66 and 67). This would tend to point to an output of some items still continuing in the Palace Workshops late in the nineteenth century.

84

Glass; of even white colour carved on each side with a pavilion nestling beneath towering cliffs, framed by a pine tree and clouds; *height: 5.7cm.*

Attributed to Beijing; 1800-1860

> PROVENANCE: Gerd Lester

The style and depth of carving and the colour tone of the material of this bottle relate very closely to that found on the enamelled glass bottles (numbers 18 and 19 above) and this bottle could well have been intended for enamelling.

84

85

85

Glass; of pale blue colour carved on front with Shou Lao unrolling a scroll decorated with a *yin-yang* symbol, the end of the scroll held by a bat, a deer to one side; *height: 4.9cm.*

1800-1880

PROVENANCE: Hugh Moss
Dr. Paula Hallett

This bottle, which is carved from a single piece of glass is probably by the same hand as that illustrated by Bob C. Stevens, *The Collector's Book of Snuff Bottles*, no. 1002. It is imitating aquamarine.

Shou Lao, the God of Longevity, is regarded as the chief of the Eight Immortals. He is usually shown with a deer and a peach. *Yin* and *yang* are ancient symbols in Chinese cosmology, the *yang* stands for the male or sky principle and the *yin* stands for the female or earth principle.

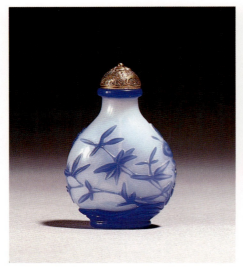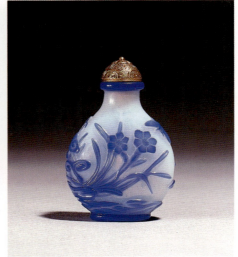

86

86

Glass; single overlay in blue on an opalescent ground with clusters of bamboo, mallow and *lingzhi* fungus growing from stylised rocks around the base; *height: 4.5cm*.

Attributed to the Beijing Palace Workshops; Qianlong period, 1736-1795

    PROVENANCE: Dr. Paula Hallett

This bottle is carved in a low relief style characteristic of a large group of snuff bottles with *Qianlong* marks in the National Palace Museum, Taiwan.[1] It also compares closely in style to a similarly marked glass overlay censer in the Palace Museum, Beijing[2].

Rarely in the history of art has there been a period comparable to the eighteenth century in China, when three successive powerful and rich emperors devoted considerable energy and expense to mobilising the resources of the whole country to the production of works of art. The result was an enormous quantity of items almost all of the highest quality. The stimulus of imperial patronage encouraged innovation and experiment but it also resulted in an overall coherence in style and technique. There is thus a certain range of subject matter and a manner of using the space available on any particular vessel which is consistent whatever the shape or type of vessel involved. The result was a certain 'eighteenth century look' which did not persist unaltered into the nineteenth century.

The development of this style is best documented by the vast range of reign-marked imperial porcelains available for study both in the West and in Beijing and Taiwan.

1. *Masterpieces of Chinese Snuff Bottles in the National Palace Museum*, Taiwan, p. 6.
2. Wango Weng and Yang Boda. *The Palace Museum*, Peking, p. 279, fig 184.

87

Glass; carved in graduated relief on each side in pale green with clumps of lotus and trilium rising from the waves, the decoration highlighted with streaks of russet, the details neatly incised; *height: 4.4cm*.

Attributed to Beijing; Qianlong period, 1736-1795

    PROVENANCE: Gerd Lester

This bottle is very similar in style and overall feel to the preceding example.

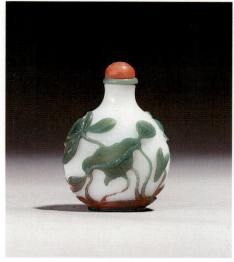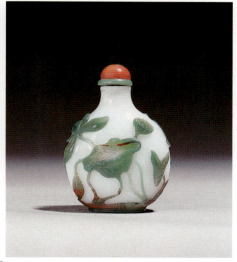

87

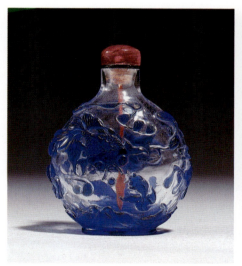

88

88

Glass; single overlay on a clear crizzled ground decorated in a bright sapphire blue with four fan-tailed carp of differing size nibbling at aquatic fronds, a band of crested waves around the base; *height: 5.9cm*.

Attributed to the Beijing Palace Workshops; Qianlong period, 1736-1795

    PROVENANCE: Emily Byrne Curtis

    EXHIBITED: Newark Museum, New Jersey, October/November 1982

Whilst it is not known exactly when the technique of carved glass overlay was introduced into the Palace Workshops there are sufficient *Qianlong*-marked examples in the Beijing and Taiwan Museums to point to the style being well established by that period.

The crizzled ground of this bottle, a common fault with early Palace glass wares, compares closely with that of number 62 above, and allows an attribution to the Palace Workshops.

A similar bottle, also decorated with fish, was exhibited at the Hong Kong Museum of Art, October 1978, *Catalogue*, no. 63.

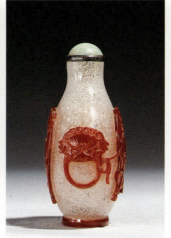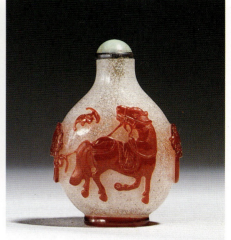

89

89

Glass; single overlay on a bubble-suffused ground depicting a prancing horse on each side, looking back at a bat, the animal tethered to a mask and ring handle on the shoulders; *height: 6cm.*

Attributed to Beijing, Qianlong period, 1736-1795

    PROVENANCE: Hugh Moss
                        Dr. Paula Hallett

    EXHIBITED: Hong Kong Museum of Art, October, 1978

    PUBLISHED: Hong Kong Museum. *Catalogue*, no. 50

As with the group of jade snuff bottles discussed above, it is difficult to draw a dividing line between objects made in the Palace workshops and items made in other centres for sending to the Palace. This particular bottle is superbly carved with movement and vitality imparted into each of the horses depicted. The additional touch of showing the animals tethered to the masks on the shoulders reveals a carver totally at ease with his medium and full of confidence. A carver of this class would almost certainly have been sent to the Palace workshops or to one of the workshops in Peking supplying the Palace.

90

Glass; single overlay on a bubble-suffused ground, carved with lotus, prunus, convolvulus and orchids in a basket extending across the base; *height: 5.8cm.*

Attributed to Beijing; Qianlong period, 1736-1795

    PROVENANCE: Bob Stevens
                        Sotheby's New York, 25th June, 1982, lot 28
                        Dr. Paula Hallett

    PUBLISHED: Bob C. Stevens. *The Collector's book of Snuff Bottles*, no. 193

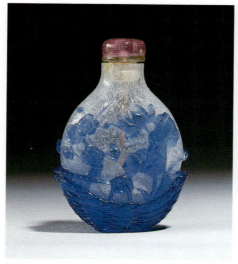

90

91

91

Glass; single overlay of red on a bubble-suffused ground, decorated on each side with a comma-filled shield suspended by interlaced ropework knotted on each shoulder; *height: 6.4cm.*

Attributed to the Beijing Palace Workshops; Qianlong period, 1736-1795

PROVENANCE: Gerd Lester

A beautifully crafted bottle with the ropework perfectly detailed and the background smoothly polished. This pattern of interlaced ropework was derived from the decoration found on ancient bronzes of the 5th and 6th centuries B.C. and was a subject often found on Palace wares. (See numbers 4 and 24 above).

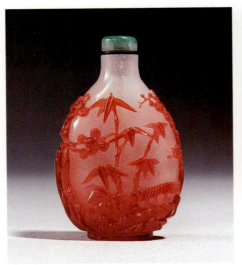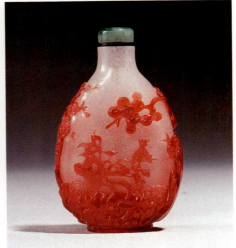

92

92

Glass; single overlay on a bubble-suffused ground, carved with 'The Three Friends', the pine, bamboo and prunus springing from rockwork beside a bridge, sprays of chrysanthemum and iris on the reverse; *height: 7.1cm.*

Attributed to Beijing; Qianlong period, 1736-1795

    PROVENANCE: K.H. Chu
                         Sotheby's London, 2nd May 1985, lot 457

The style of rockwork on this bottle compares closely with that on number 94 below, thereby pointing to possibly the same workshop for their manufacture.

'The Three Friends' were referred to by Confucius. As the three friends in winter, they do not die but remain constant and blossom before the spring comes.

93

Glass; three-coloured overlay on a bubble-suffused ground depicting numerous butterflies amidst fruiting durian, the gnarled stalk forming the base; *height: 5.4cm.*

Attributed to Beijing; Qianlong period, 1736-1795

    PROVENANCE: Eric Young
                         Sotheby's London, 3rd March, 1987, lot 12

The style of carving on this bottle, particularly the treatment of the butterfly wings and the lipped edges of the leaves, is very close to that found on eighteenth century cinnabar lacquer carving.

The durian is a fruit much prized in the East for its sweet flavour and much hated for its foul smell.

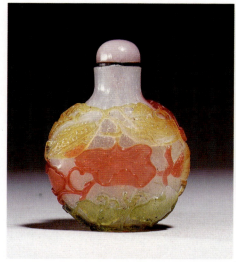

93

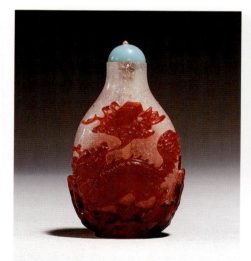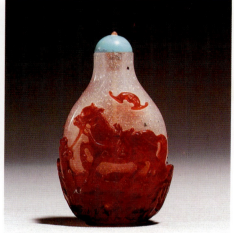

94

94

Glass; single overlay on a bubble-suffused ground with a prancing horse tethered to a post beneath a swooping bat, a kylin on the reverse exhaling a cloud to envelope a box, the base encircled by pierced rockwork; *height: 6.7cm.*

Attributed to Beijing; Qianlong period, 1736-1795

PROVENANCE: Janos Szekeres
Sotheby's New York, 27th October, 1986, lot 32

The style of the carving of the horse on this bottle relates very closely to that of the horse on number 89 above and the rockwork compares closely to that on number 92, and it is possible that these three bottles were made in the same workshop.

The kylin is one of a group of the four Chinese supernatural creatures, along with the dragon, the tortoise and the phoenix. It symbolises a large family of children. Legend has it that the kylin will not step on any living thing and it is therefore a symbol of goodness, as well.

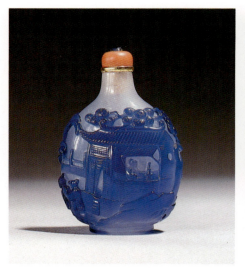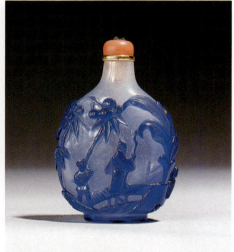

95

95

Glass; single overlay of blue on an opaque ground, carved with a sage walking across a bridge, followed by an assistant, towards a figure seated in front of a vase within a pavilion, the scene framed by pine, bamboo and a palm tree; *height: 6.1cm*.

Attributed to Beijing; Qianlong period, 1736-1795

PROVENANCE: Gerd Lester

The style of carving on this bottle is more rounded than that of the preceding examples, but in the fluidity of its design and the carefulness of its finishing it belongs to the eighteenth century.

96

Glass; an overlay of seven differing colours, carved to depict nine writhing dragons each in a differing attitude, one forming the base; *height: 6.6cm*.

Attributed to Beijing; Qianlong period, 1736-1795

PROVENANCE: Emily Byrne Curtis

EXHIBITED: Newark Museum, New Jersey, October/November 1982

The dragon is one of China's most complex and multi-tiered symbols. It is the symbol of young male vigour and fertility and the symbol of the Emperor as Son of Heaven. In contrast to its standing in the West, the dragon is viewed as a benign being in China. Nine dragons are of particular imperial significance and there are two famous nine dragon walls in Beijing, one within the Forbidden City and one just to the north.

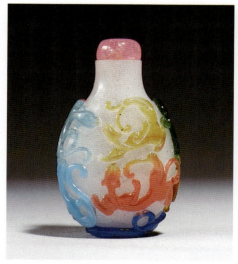

96

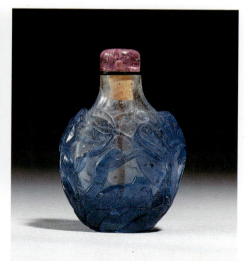

97

97

Glass; single overlay of dark blue on a clear ground carved with three geese swimming beneath lotus; *height: 5.3cm.*

Attributed to Beijing; Qianlong period, 1736-1795

The goose has become linked in Chinese thought with the famous calligrapher, Wang Xizhi, who is said to have likened the supple line of their necks to the best brush-strokes in the art of calligraphy[1].

1. G. Tsang and H. Moss. *Arts From the Scholar's Studio*, no. 56.

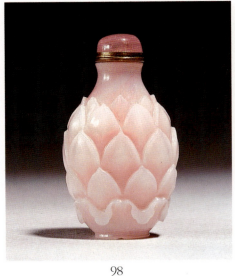

98

99

98

Glass; of pinkish tone carved overall with overlapping tiers of lotus petals; *height: 5.7cm.*

Attributed to Beijing; Qianlong period, 1736-1795

The carver in this case has used the whitish outer layer of the glass with great skill to provide a difference in the shading of the lotus petals. This subject was popular in the eighteenth century (see the jade example, number 28 above).

99

Glass; single overlay of pale orange on an amber-coloured ground, depicting three bats in graduated relief enclosing a single tasselled cash; *height: 5.5cm.*

1770-1820

    PROVENANCE: The Belfort Collection

An elegantly conceived example in an unusual combination of colours.

100

Glass; a five-colour overlay on a clear ground, depicting a bat, its wings displayed, grasping a *lingzhi* spray above a *shou* medallion in the centre; *height: 5.9cm.*

1770-1820

    PROVENANCE: Hugh Moss
                     The Belfort Collection

This bottle acquires a dramatic impact from the skilful use of the clear background combined with the minimum of carved decoration. The *shou* medallion is a stylised representation of the character for 'longevity'.

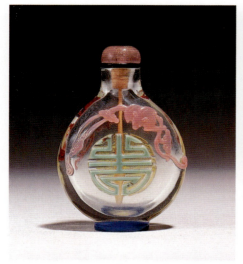
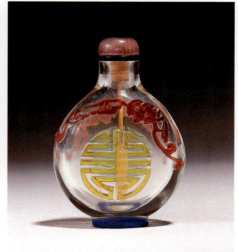

100

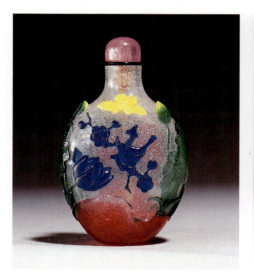
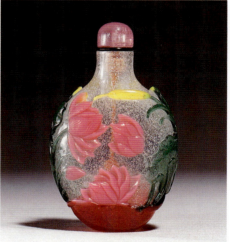

101

101

Glass; a five-colour overlay on a bubble-suffused ground depicting clusters of lotus and millet rising from a curled leaf around the foot, the reverse with a bird and a butterfly on prunus; *height: 6.3cm.*

1770-1820

    PROVENANCE: Eric Young
                        Sotheby's London, 3rd March, 1987, lot 24

Although the quality of carving on this example compares well with that of the preceding examples, the introduction of brighter colours points towards a slightly later date of manufacture.

102   103

102

Glass; single overlay of white on dark blue, depicting six lilies; *height: 6cm.*

1780-1860

    PROVENANCE: B.T. Lyons
                     Sotheby's London, 20th April, 1982, lot 15

A very rare and elegant combination of colours. The lily is reputed to be the plant which makes one forget one's troubles. It is also known as 'The bringer of sons' and so is given to young women on their marriage.

103

Glass; single overlay of rich green tone on a white ground, carved on each side to depict a dragon writhing in and out of an archaic *bi* disc, mask and ring handles on the shoulders; *height: 7.6cm.*

1770-1820

The *bi* disc was a jade ornament in use from archaic times until the end of the Qing Dynasty as a symbol of heaven.

104

Glass; double overlay of blue on ruby-red, carved in deep relief on one side with a pavilion standing on stilts above crested waves and on the reverse with a recumbent buffalo resting beneath a pine tree, the sides with mask and ring handles on top of bats and clouds; *height: 5.8cm.*

1780-1850

    PROVENANCE: H.G. Beasley
                     Mac Beasley
                     Sotheby's London, 2nd July, 1984, lot 13
                     K.H. Chu

The depth of the overlay on this example is remarkable and the carver has succeeded in maintaining control of the design and the polishing, throughout.

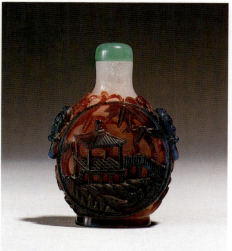

104

105

105

Glass; single overlay of lapis-blue on a bubble-suffused ground, depicting a crested egret wading beneath clusters of lotus and millet; *height: 6.2cm*.

1770-1850

This bottle is stylistically similar to number 97 above, although slightly stiffer in its execution.

106   107

106

Glass; single overlay of white on a crizzled royal blue ground, carved on each side with a coiled *chilong* and on the shoulders with bats; *height: 5.6cm*.

1750-1820

PROVENANCE: Gerd Lester

107

Glass; two-colour overlay on a bubble-suffused ground, the overlay left in its uncarved state; *height: 6.2cm*.

1770-1850

PROVENANCE: Sotheby's London, 2nd May, 1985, lot 373

This bottle is of interest because the overlay has been left uncarved. It demonstrates one of the stages in the technique of overlay carving. First the basic body is blown into a mould. The body is then applied with layers of molten glass in whatever colour the final decoration is intended and when this layer has hardened it is carved away in cameo style down to the original surface of the body.

108

Glass; single overlay of red on an opalescent white ground, carved with twelve magpies swooping above clusters of lotus rising from the waves; *height: 6.7cm*.

1770-1820

The call of the magpie heralds good news or the arrival of a guest. A picture of twelve magpies expresses twelve good wishes.

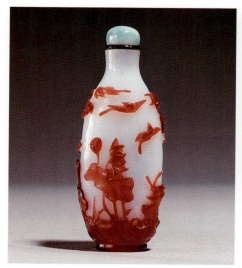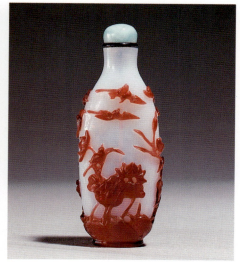

108

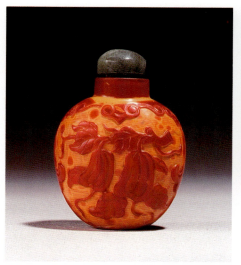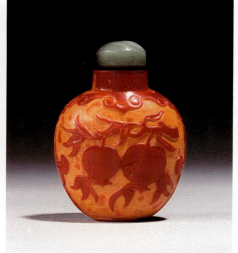

109

109

Glass; yellow and red glass, imitating realgar, carved on one side with fruiting pomegranate and on the reverse with a cluster of melons, beneath a *ruyi* head collar around the neck; *height: 5.5cm.*

1800-1860

PROVENANCE: Gerd Lester

Realgar (arsenic bisulphide) was an important substance in Daoist alchemical practice. Because of its fragility as a material and its toxicity it was extensively imitated in glass, its colours being widely admired[1].

1. G. Tsang and H. Moss. *Arts From the Scholar's Studio*, no. 94.

110

110

Glass; single overlay of sapphire blue on a white ground, carved on front with clusters of flowering lotus springing from the waves, the reverse with a stylised inscription followed by the seal *Songxian* (Pine Pavilion); *height: 5.1cm.*

1800-1859

PROVENANCE: Hugh Moss

The inscription on the back of this bottle may be read as follows; *in the shadow of the setting sun the leaves of the lotus turn to red.*

The Pine Pavilion belonged to the mid-Qing poet, Zhang Weiping (1780-1859) and use of the hall name implies that the poem was by him and the bottle made for him[1].

The bottle is of superb quality showing that the eighteenth century did not enjoy exclusive rights in this area.

1. See A. Hummel. *Eminent Chinese of The Ch'ing Period.*

111

Glass; single overlay of white on dark blue, carved with lotus, a single leaf covering the back; *height: 5.2cm.*

1770-1850

PROVENANCE: Hugh Moss
Dr. Paula Hallett
Sotheby's New York, 27th June, 1986, lot 20

The treatment of the leaf on the back of this bottle is highly original and the finish is impeccable, right down to the carefully shaped footrim.

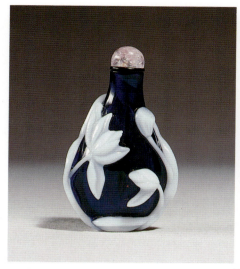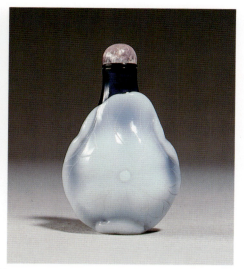

111

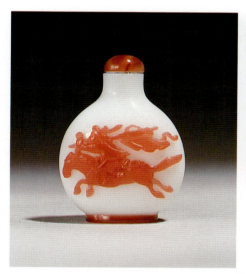

112

112

Glass; single overlay of pinkish-red on a white ground, carved on front with a Manchu bannerman galloping, the reverse with an eight-character couplet, *the finger of heaven's majesty makes a clean sweep of evil influences*, and two seals; *height: 5.2cm.*

1800-1860

PROVENANCE: The Ko Collection
                      J.& J. Collection
                      Hugh Moss
                      Dr. Paula Hallett
                      Sotheby's New York, 27th June, 1986, lot 23

This is a rare subject to find on glass, although it is often found depicted on the cameo-style chalcedony bottles which date from the first half of the nineteenth century. The subject is carved with great vigour and movement.

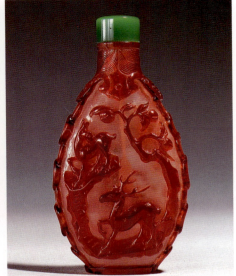

113

113

Glass; single overlay of red on an opaque ground, carved on one side with a figure seated on a rock, playing the flute, the reverse with a deer on a rock looking down at its mate, the shoulders each with a chain of interlinked rings extending from the mouth to the foot; *height: 8.8cm.*

1820-1880

PROVENANCE: Adolph Silver
Sotheby's London, 6th March 1979, lot 74

The device of interlinked chains on the shoulders of this bottle is worthy of note.

114

Glass; six-colour overlay on a bubble-suffused ground, decorated with eighteen monkeys cavorting in differing attitudes; *height: 5.8cm.*

1780-1860

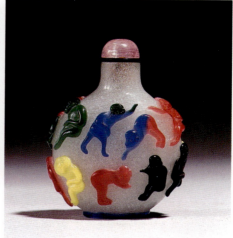

114

115

115

Glass; single overlay of green on dark blue, carved on front with a praying mantis amongst fruiting pods and on the reverse with a cricket on a cabbage; *height: 6.3cm.*

1800-1880

PROVENANCE: Hugh Moss
Dr. Paula Hallett

Another very unusual combination of colours crisply executed. The cricket is a summer insect which symbolises pluck and fighting spirit. They were often kept in specially crafted cages so that their song could be heard.

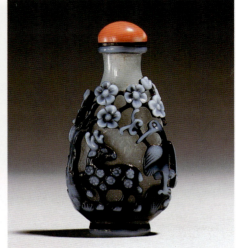

116

116

Glass; double overlay of white and black on a bubble-suffused ground, carved on one side with a prancing tethered horse and on the reverse with a deer and a stork beneath a pine tree; *height: 5.7cm.*

1840-1880

117

Glass; a five-colour overlay of slender *chilong* and scattered sprays enclosing two *shou* medallions; *height: 7.9cm.*

1800-1860

PROVENANCE: Gerd Lester

Bottles of this distinctive group have been long attributed by collectors to the workshops of the Yuan Family in Beijing. Whilst there can be little doubt that these bottles are the product of a single workshop, there is no convincing evidence as to its name or its whereabouts. Nevertheless they are of high quality both in the conception of their designs and in their crafting.

117

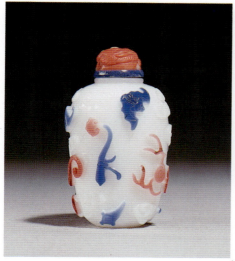

118

118

Glass; two-colour overlay on a white ground, carved and overlaid with a scaly dragon chasing a 'flaming pearl' amidst swooping bats and cloud billows; *height: 4.7cm.*

1800-1860

PROVENANCE: Hugh Moss

This bottle is unusual in that the body has first been carved with the designs, some of which have then been highlighted with overlay colours.

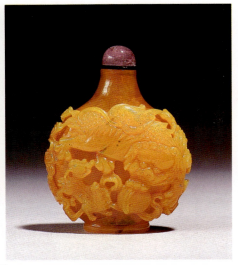

119

120

119

Glass; single overlay of yellow on an amber-coloured ground, carved on each side with a lion and its cub playing with a brocade ball; *height: 5.8cm.*

1780-1850

The incised detail on this bottle is unusually crisply executed, and relates to a specific workshop style. The colour combination is rare.

120

Glass; five-colour overlay on a turquoise ground, carved on each side with a bunch of lotus and millet; *height: 6.1cm.*

1840-1880

PROVENANCE: Gerd Lester

The style and subject matter of this bottle compare very closely with that of the *Guangxu*-marked carved bottle, number 83 above.

121

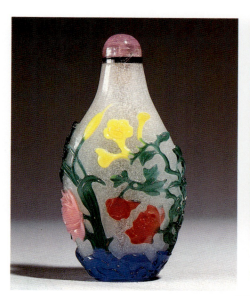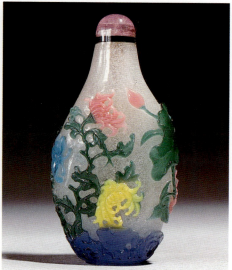

122

121

Glass; single overlay of red on a bubble-suffused ground, depicting a figure riding a camel and smoking a pipe, the reverse depicting a man and a dog watching a figure shooting an arrow at a bird; *height: 7.9cm.*

1800-1860

Both sides of this bottle depict very unusual subjects similar in style to those found on the group of cameo carved chalcedony bottles.

122

Glass; six-colour overlay on a bubble-suffused ground, carved overall with flowering sprays of peony, chrysanthemum, lotus, millet and magnolia rising from rockwork; *height: 8.3cm.*

1780-1850

123

124

123

Glass; double overlay of white and green on a pink ground, depicting the various stages in the cycle of the silkworm, from cocoon to moth; *height: 6cm*.

1800-1880

    PUBLISHED: H. Moss. *Chinese Snuff Bottles*, No. 5, p. 117

A very rare subject on snuff bottles; only four others have been recorded and they are almost certainly by the same hand.

124

Glass; single overlay of cinnabar-red on a white ground, carved on each side with four boys with two heads forming a linked medallion, one boy holding musical pipes (*sheng*), another holding a lotus spray; *height: 6.6cm*.

Possibly Yangzhou; 1850-1900

The decoration on this bottle represents the four-fold happiness. It is also an allusion to the Daoist Classic, the Dao Teqing.

125

Glass; single overlay on a white ground, carved in low relief with a deity standing in the clouds pouring pearls out of an alms bowl towards a dragon swimming on the crested waves below, a second deity to one side riding a tiger, flanked by a seal inscription reading *feng yun ji hui; height: 6.9cm.*

Yangzhou; 1850-1900

    PROVENANCE: Hugh Moss

The inscription may be read '*a gathering of heroes*' (literally a gathering of the wind and the clouds).

Yangzhou is a district in the coastal province of Jiangsu. During the nineteenth century its was a prosperous commercial centre and it supported its own artistic community. Among those active at this period was a group of painters called the Eight Eccentrics of Yangzhou who broke new ground in Chinese art.

Gerard Tsang[1] has traced the development of the Yangzhou glass bottles to this style of painting. Several bottles in the group are known with artists seals and some bear cyclical dates[2]. The earliest reference to glass overlay bottles which Tsang found was by Chau Chixu in his commentary on Zhao Zhijian's *Leisure Inquires on Snuff*, dated 1893. In addition, there are three *Yangzhou* bottles in the Salting Bequest to the Victoria and Albert Museum, London, which were already in the Museum by 1895, having been collected during the preceding ten years or so. These particular bottles are of the highest quality thereby allowing one to assume that the workshop would have been established for several years before they were purchased.

A bottle with a cyclical date equivalent to A.D. 1881 was exhibited at the Hong Kong Museum of Art, October, 1978, *Catalogue*, no. 242.

The bottle illustrated represents the *Yangzhou* School at its best. It is carved with the low relief overlay typical of the School but in this case the control and delicacy of the carving, particularly where it has been left in different depths to suggest shading, is of outstanding quality.

1. G. Tsang. 'Yangzhou Seal Bottles', *Journal* of the I.C.S.B.S., June 1979.
2. See number 126 below, which is dated 1880.

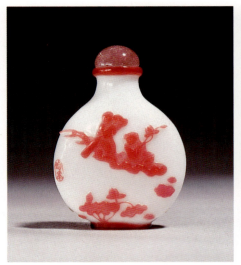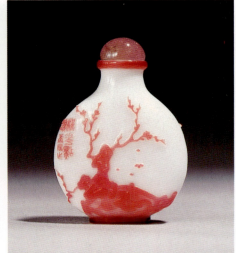

126

126

Glass; single overlay of ruby-red on a white ground, carved in low relief on one side with a maiden reclining against an ornamental rock on a terrace, a seal inscription to one side, *prunus blossom marks the forehead, made in the year gengchen* (1880), the reverse with two figures paddling a tree boat through clumps of lotus, a seal *Junting*, (the name of a pavilion), on the shoulders; *height: 6.1cm.*

Yangzhou; 1880

    PROVENANCE: Gerd Lester

Another bottle of the highest quality. The colour of the overlay and the style of carving compare so closely with that of one the Salting bottles in the Victoria and Albert Museum, that they could well be by the same hand.

127

Glass; single overlay of reddish-brown highlighting low relief carved decoration including several bronze vessels, a *weiqi* board, a brushpot full of scholar's articles and a miniature tree, inscribed in overlaid relief with a wish for *eight thousand springs and autumns* and with a seal *ciwan*, (*for my own pleasure*); *height: 5.7cm.*

Yangzhou; 1850-1900

    PROVENANCE: Hugh Moss
                      The Belfort Collection

    EXHIBITED: Hong Kong Museum of Art, October, 1978
                      Arcade Chaumet, Paris, June 1982, *Catalogue*, no. 121

    PUBLISHED: Hong Kong Museum. *Catalogue*, no. 243
                      V. Jutheau. *Tabatières Chinoises*, p. 66, figs. 1 and 2

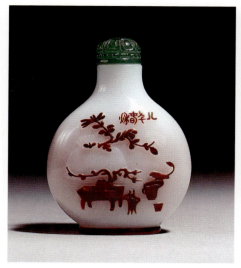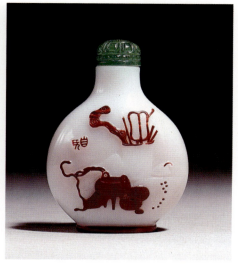

127

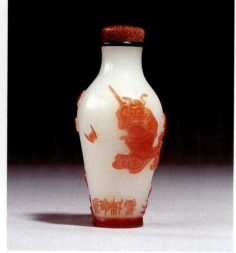

128

128

Glass; single overlay of pale red on a white ground, depicting Zhonggui, the Demon Queller, standing on a cloud, a demon bearing him a tray with a ewer and a cup, a pierced rock around the base, flanked by a seal inscription *precious trinket of the Cloud Study; height: 6.2cm.*

Yangzhou; 1850-1900

PROVENANCE: Janos Szekeres
                         Sotheby's New York, 27th October, 1986, lot 63

EXHIBITED: New Orleans Museum of Art, October, 1980

PUBLISHED: *Journal* of the I.C.S.B.S., June 1975, p. 9

Zhonggui is revered as the exorcist *par excellence* in China and his picture is hung up at the end of the year or on the 5th day of the 5th month in order to scare away demons and evil spirits. He was well known for his penchent for getting drunk as is alluded to in the design on this bottle.

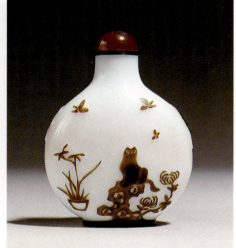

129

129

Glass; single overlay of brown on a white ground, decorated on one side with birds pecking at millet beneath a bowl of fruit and a spray of blossom, a seal inscription *sui sui ping an* (peace year after year) on the shoulders, the reverse with a cat on a tall rock looking up at hovering butterflies, a twin fish on each shoulder; *height: 5.9cm*.

Yangzhou; 1850-1900

  PROVENANCE: Gerd Lester

The words for 'cat' and 'octogenarian,' *mao*, are phonetically close, so a picture of a cat and butterflies expresses the wish that the recipient should live to be seventy or eighty (butterflies symbolise the numeral, seventy).

130

Glass; single overlay of red on a pale coffee-coloured ground carved to depict a crane with a wooden rod in its bill, flying towards the sun setting beneath the waves, the reverse with bats swooping around a jagged upright rock; *height: 6.3cm*.

Yangzhou; 1850-1900

It is rare to find a bottle from this School with both carved and overlay decoration. In this case the bulk of the design has been finely carved with the minimum of red overlay skilfully used to provide subtle highlights.

The scene of the crane on this bottle reflects the saying 'one more counter for the pavilion by the sea.' This is an allusion to the legend of the three ageless Daoists and therefore expresses a wish to the recipient for a long life. Such layers of meaning would only have been understood by a well educated person and the decoration on this bottle is a good example of the type of hidden messages in art which delighted the literati.

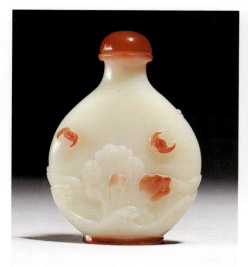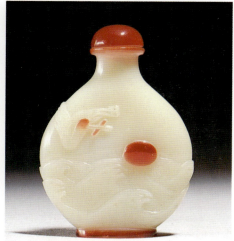

130

131

131

Glass; a double overlay of cinnabar-red on green, on a coffee-coloured ground decorated on one side with two tethered Buddhist lions and on the reverse with several more, some emerging from rocks, encircling a brocade ball; *height: 5.7cm.*

Yangzhou; 1850-1900

    PROVENANCE: Gerd Lester

A rare example from this School of double overlay decoration.

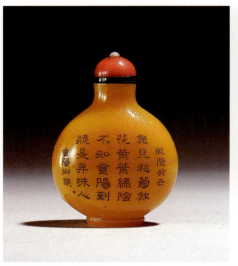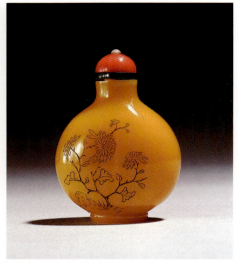

132

132

Glass; imperial yellow incised on one side with an imperial poem and the inscription *Qianlong gui chou* (Qianlong A.D. 1793), the reverse with a spray of chrysanthemum springing from a rock; *height: 5.3cm.*

Attributed to the Beijing Palace Workshops; 1793-1830

    PROVENANCE: Hugh Moss
                       Dr. Paula Hallett

An enormous number of artefacts, both antique and contemporary, were inscribed during the Qianlong reign with the Emperor's poems. The practice of inscribing these poems continued after the Emperor's death often together with a date, but such a date usually referred to the time of writing of the poem rather than the date it was inscribed on the particular object.

Judging by the slight stiffness in the floral decoration on this bottle it is possible that a poem written by the Emperor in 1793 was inscribed at a slightly later date.

133

Glass; of flattened rectangular form, incised on front with a gnarled spray of peach blossom and on the reverse with a lengthy inscription and the signature *Baimen Hongbin* followed by the seal *zhou* and a cyclical date equivalent to A.D. 1902; *height: 6.2cm.*

By Zhou Honglai; Nanjing; 1902

    PROVENANCE: Hugh Moss

Zhou Honglai was one of a number of artists who specialised in incising miniature inscriptions on snuff bottles, ivory screens and ivory plaques between 1900 and 1950. Zhou was from Nanjing and his known works date from 1902 to 1909. Two bottles dated, respectively, 1904 and 1909, were exhibited at the Hong Kong Museum of Art, October, 1978, *Catalogue*, nos. 244 and 245.

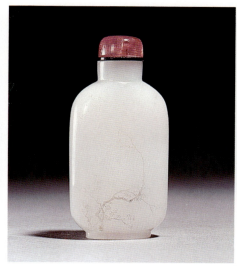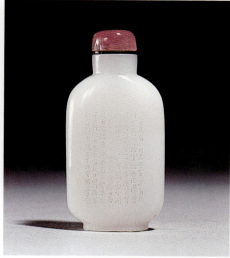

133

134

134

Glass; of rounded rectangular form, incised on one side with a peach tree in blossom flanked by an inscription, and on the reverse with a lengthy inscription and the signature *Zhou Honglai, Nanjing* and a cyclical date equivalent to 1903, followed by the seal *zhou*; *height: 4.9cm.*

By Zhou Honglai; Nanjing; 1903

Rock Crystal
and Chalcedony

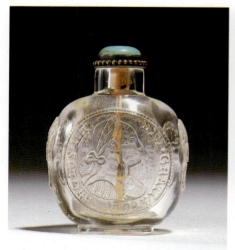  

135

Rock crystal; colourless; carved in low relief with both sides of a Spanish silver dollar, the front with the obverse inscription DEI GRATIA. 1798. CAROLUS IIII.; the back with the reverse inscription HISPAN. ETIND. REX. M. 8R FM, mask and ring handles on the shoulders; *height: 5.6cm.*

1800 — 1850

PROVENANCE: Hugh Moss
The Belfort Collection

EXHIBITED: Hong Kong Museum of Art, October 1978
Arcade Chaumet, Paris, June 1982, *Catalogue*, no. 181

PUBLISHED: H. Moss. *Chinese Snuff Bottles of the Silica or Quartz Group*, no. 202
Hong Kong Museum. *Catalogue*, no. 180

The Spanish silver dollar was common currency in the sea ports of China throughout the nineteenth century. The letter M on this bottle indicates that the coin it was copying was minted for Spain's Mexican territories[1]. This particular coin began to loose popularity by about 1850 and it is thus reasonable to postulate a date for the bottle of 1800-1850.

Snuff bottles imitating coins were made in some quantity, mainly of chalcedony or rock crystal, but it is rare to find an example with the inscriptions as accurately rendered as on this bottle.

The crispness and quality of the carving is unusual, as are the mask handles on the shoulders, and this would tend to confirm the dating.

1. H. Moss. *Chinese Snuff Bottles of the Silica* or *Quartz Group*, p. 75.

136

136

Rock crystal; colourless; in the form of a double-gourd, the upper bulb carved in low relief with the character *da*, the lower bulb with the character *ji*, the centre encircled by a brocade cloth, knotted on one side and incised overall with an interlaced pattern; *height: 6.3cm.*

1780-1850

PROVENANCE: Ralph Hult
Mr. & Mrs L. Kardos
Sotheby's New York, 1st July 1985, lot 88

Rock crystal was readily available to the Chinese throughout the Qing period, mainly from Fujian Province[1]. This bottle is crafted with great care, the exterior being polished perfectly smooth and the interior hollowed almost paper thin, an extremely difficult exercise, particularly on the rounded walls of the lower bulb. From the few documented examples of rock crystal and chalcedony bottles[2], it appears that the first half of the nineteenth century was the high-point for well made examples of these materials.

1. H. Moss. *Chinese Snuff Bottles of the Silica or Quartz Group*, p. 6.
2. See numbers 141 and 142 below.

137

Glass; colourless; incised on the interior with a pine tree on each side, with fishermen to one side, an inscription on the shoulders, *engraved by Wang Junlin in a winter month, 1904, in imitation of Nantian Laoren's[1] style*, the side with the pine tree inscribed, *the old dragon snatches the luminous pearl from the dark night; height: 5.8cm.*

Interior decoration by Wang Junlin; dated 1904

PROVENANCE: Arthur Gadsby
The Belfort Collection

EXHIBITED: Hong Kong Museum of Art, 1977, *Catalogue*, no. 50

This is the only recorded example of a snuff bottle incised on the interior. Nothing is known about the artist, Wang Junlin but he used an old bottle, and incised the decoration with brilliant skill, probably using a diamond-tipped instrument.

1. Nantian Laoren is the fancy name of the Qing painter Yun Shaoping (1633-1690).

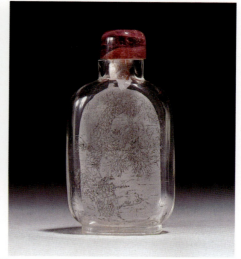

137

138

138

Rock crystal; brown; carved as a cicada with wings folded, the details of the membrane neatly incised; *height: 5.3cm.*

1780-1880

PROVENANCE: Dr. Paula Hallett

EXHIBITED: Hong Kong Musuem of Art, October 1978

PUBLISHED: Hong Kong Museum. *Catalogue*, no. 189

The cicada symbolises immortality because of its cycle of apparent death and rebirth. It is one of the most ancient of Chinese decorative motifs being found as early as the Shang Dynasty, c. 1600-1100 B.C., on archaic bronze vessels, but it is rare to find a snuff bottle of this form.

139

140

139

Rock crystal; colourless; suffused with slender reddish needles of rutile; *height: 6cm.*

1780-1850

PROVENANCE: Sotheby's London, 2nd May 1985, lot 401

Rock crystal with this type of inclusion is much rarer than that found with black tourmaline inclusions.

The shape of this bottle, a flattened rectangle supported on a neatly finished footrim, compares closely with that belonging to a group of jadeite snuff bottles of varying shades of apple-green colour. This particular shade and type of jadeite is found, as well, on a series of bowls dating from the late Qianlong and Jiaqing periods[1], thus pointing to a date for the jadeite bottles and their crystal counterparts of around the turn of the eighteenth and the nineteenth century.

1. Wang Yi. *Life in the Forbidden City*, p. 195, fig. 279.

140

Rock crystal; colourless with hair-like inclusions of black tourmaline; *height: 5.8cm.*

1750-1850

PROVENANCE: Cyril Green
Hugh Moss
Count Kurt Blucher Von Wahlstatt
V. Meglys

PUBLISHED: H. Moss. *Chinese Snuff Bottles of the Silica or Quartz Group*, p. 11, fig. 15
H. Moss. *Snuff Bottles of China*, no.87

A number of carvings in this material, which date from the eighteenth century, are in the National Palace Museum, Taiwan. This, together with the rounded shape of the bottle, a shape favoured in the eighteenth century for snuff bottles, allows the parameters for dating to be extended further back than those of the rectangular example, no 139 above.

141

Rock crystal; colourless; incised and gilded on one side with a crane pecking at *lingzhi* fungus on a lakeside beneath a pine tree, the reverse with a deer prancing beneath rockwork, an inscription *Qianlong yuzhi bingwu* on the shoulders, the base inscribed *Daoguang jiyou xingyouheng tang zhi* (*made for the Hall of Constancy in 1849 in the Daoguang reign*); *height: 6.7cm.*

Bottle, 1849
Incised decoration added later

PROVENANCE:	Robert Hall
	Emily Byrne Curtis
PUBLISHED:	Michel Beurdeley & M.T.Lambert-Brouillet.
	L'Eunuque aux Trois Joyeaux, p.p. 158-165, nos. 114-117

The Xinghouheng Tang (usually translated as 'The Hall of Constancy'), belonged to the fifth Prince, Ding, Zaichuan, who died in 1854. He was a great-great-grandson of the Qianlong Emperor and inherited the Princedom from his father in 1836[1]. Educated at the Palace School for Princes he occupied various official posts.

Zaichuan was a keen collector and connoisseur of works of art, including glass and jade waterpots, several snuff bottles, a group of moulded gourds and similar objects for the scholars studio. All of these bear his hall mark, often with a date, as well.[2]

This particular bottle is typical of the stone bottles found in this studio. It is perfectly finished and hollowed paper thin, and it demonstrates that bottles of the highest quality were still being made half way through the nineteenth century[2]. The incised decoration was probably added at some time during the artistic and technical renaissance of the post 1949 era in China.

1. G. Tsang and H. Moss. *Arts From the Scholar's Studio*, no. 108.
2. See also number 33 above and number 166 below.

142

Chalcedony; of pale mushroom colour, the base incised *Yi Jin zhai (Appreciation of Imperial Favour Studio)*; *height: 5.3cm.*

1770-1823

PROVENANCE: Hugh Moss
                     Dr. Paula Hallett
                     Sotheby's, New York, 2nd December, 1985, lot 79

EXHIBITED: Hong Kong Museum of Art, October, 1978

PUBLISHED: Hong Kong Museum. *Catalogue*, no. 44

The 'Appreciation of Imperial Favour Studio' belonged to Yongxing, the first Prince Cheng, eleventh son of the Qianlong Emperor. Like his relative, Prince Ding[1], he kept there numerous carefully chosen works of art, and his dates are established[2].

From the few recorded snuff bottles belonging to these two princes, it appears that they both favoured beautifully crafted plain bottles made of relatively common stones such as rock crystal or chalcedony. We have already seen that the materials favoured by the Court in the eighteenth century tended to be more precious, such as glass or jade, and the trend towards a less valuable material was consistent with the ideals of the scholar class which wielded more influence during the first half of the nineteenth century, after the decline of Imperial and official influence.

This group, to which both princes belonged, took pleasure in recognising that great works of art did not necessarily have to be made from expensive materials and indeed the more simple or common the material, the more merit it would impart to the object in question.

This bottle is made with the utmost care. The base is countersunk and the rim of the neck is lipped. It is hollowed out almost to a paper thinness and is virtually weightless, thereby allowing the light to shine through. A stone, common and worthless in itself has been transformed into an object of wonder to be admired and to give inspiration.

1. See number 141 above.
2. See Hummel, p. 962.

143

144

143

Chalcedony; of rich honey colour, supported on a countersunk base, the mouth with a lipped rim; *height: 5.5cm.*

1770-1830

    PROVENANCE: Hugh Moss
                        Dr. Paula Hallett
                        Sotheby's New York, 27th June 1986, lot 40

This bottle, although uninscribed, is so close to the previous example in its shape and the quality of its manufacture that it is likely to have been made in the same workshops.

144

Agate; of pale greyish tone encircled around the centre by a double russet line; *height: 6.2cm.*

1750-1850

    PROVENANCE: Gerd Lester

Agate is the variety of chalcedony which includes banded markings and is a term which should properly only be applied to this particular type.

The material of which this bottle is made has a translucent metallic sheen which adds greatly to its appeal. Full use has been made of this quality and the bottle is superbly hollowed out, allowing the light to shine through. Once again, perfection of craftsmanship and material have combined to lift the completed product above the level of mere utility.

145

146

145

Chalcedony; of honey colour and circular section; *height: 5.7cm*.

1770-1850

Another example of a beautifully crafted bottle. The footrim is neatly finished and the hollowing out process has left a cloudy pattern on the thin walls of the vessel which creates a beguiling translucent effect.

146

Agate; of honey colour suffused with numerous white markings, mask and ring handles on the shoulders; *height: 6.1cm*.

    PROVENANCE: Hugh Moss
                        Count Kurt Blucher Von Wahlstatt
                        V. Meglys

    PUBLISHED: H. Moss. *Snuff Bottles of the Silica or Quartz Group*, p. 16, fig. 30
                        H. Moss. *Snuff Bottles of China*, cover & no. 40

An unusual variety of agate, sometimes known as 'macaroni', because of the shape of the inclusions, obtained by cutting the stone at an angle to the parallel bandings.

147

Chalcedony; pale grey tone with darker inclusions carved to depict a figure leading a deer towards a pierced rock, a pine tree extending across the shoulders, the reverse with a short inscription, *picture of obtaining high rank*, in raised relief, enclosed by tiered and serrated rockwork; *height: 4.5cm.*

Suzhou School; 1730-1830

PROVENANCE: Kenneth Woolcombe-Boyce
Hugh Moss
Blair Hills

PUBLISHED: Hugh Moss. *Snuff Bottles of the Silica or Quartz Group*, p. 67, fig. 176
Hugh Moss. *Chinese Snuff Bottles*, No. 2, front cover

The origins and basic characteristics of the Suzhou school have been briefly discussed in relation to the jade examples in the Catalogue[1]. However, the full range and quality of those characteristics is, perhaps, better demonstrated by the examples in chalcedony, in which the greater varieties of tone and inclusion in the material itself often gave further scope to the craftsmen involved in the manufacture to demonstrate their virtuosity.

This bottle is an example of Suzhou virtuosity at its best. Each inclusion in the stone, no matter how small, has been used to add something to the overall design. The tiny patch of black hair on the figure is a particular touch of brilliance. Nevertheless, virtuosity in itself does not create a work of art. The essence of this bottle, the intangible aura which raises it from the realms of superb craftsmanship to that of art, resides not in the physical skill of the lapidary, but in the sense of movement and naturalness which he has managed to impart into the picture. For myself, the figure is trudging home wearily, his head bent in fatigue, his feet trailing in the dust, whilst the deer prances merrily behind. A perfect encapsulation of the drudgery of work and the innocence of the animal kingdom. However, as with all great works of art, others will no doubt have a completely different interpretation.

1. See number 36 above.

148

148

Chalcedony; pale honey colour with darker inclusions on front carved to depict a bearded figure in a court hat, peering across pierced rocks towards the sea, an inscription on the shoulders, a *wutong* tree above, the reverse with the doors of a pavilion wreathed by clouds; *height: 4.9cm.*

Suzhou School; 1730-1830

    PROVENANCE: Hugh Moss
                      Robert Hall

    PUBLISHED: Hugh Moss. *Snuff Bottles of the Silica or Quartz Group*, p. 68, fig. 178

This bottle exhibits a rare feature for the Suzhou School. The leaves of the tree, instead of being carved, have been cross-hatched, giving an air of remarkable but abstracted realism and suggesting the play of light through the foliage. The reverse, with its cloud scrolls, typical of this School, has a large area of reddish-brown which has been brilliantly used to depict the doors of the pavilion, another example of the Suzhou carver using every nuance of colour to add to the design.

149

Chalcedony; of honey colour carved on front using darker inclusions to depict a sage painting on a rock, his assistant nearby, carrying a box, the reverse with swirling serrated rockwork; *height: 5.9cm.*

Suzhou School; 1750-1830

    PROVENANCE: Hugh Moss

    PUBLISHED: Hugh Moss. *Snuff Bottles of the Silica or Quartz Group*, p. 65, no. 169

This bottle and the one following are part of a very small group within the Suzhou School which exhibits certain similarities both in the manner in which the stone has been used and within the material itself. The darker inclusions in the stone are slightly broken and dappled and match exactly in tone. The carving of the subject matter is unusually fluid and in a low, flattened relief which is unusual for the School as a whole[1]. It may well transpire, when more detailed research has been done, that one will be able to discern the work of particular artists by such similarities in style and materials.

1. Another example of this group was sold at Sotheby's London, 28th April 1987, lot 658.

149

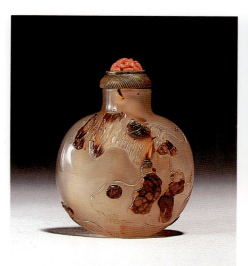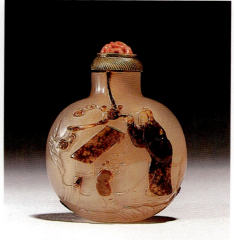

150

150

Chalcedony; of honey colour with darker inclusions on front carved in low relief to depict a sage plucking a sprig of blossom, a boy standing by a table to one side, the reverse with a figure seated in front of a pot, his attendant nearby, serrated rockwork above; *height: 4.9cm*.

Suzhou School; 1750-1830

    PROVENANCE: Gerd Lester

In the style of its carving and the tone of the material this bottle could well be by the same artist as no. 149 above. In the perfection of its finishing and polishing, with no traces of drill marks, it exhibits another characteristic of the School as a whole.

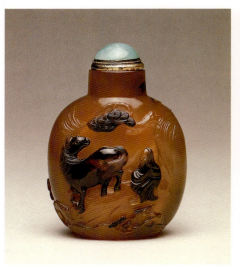 

151

Chalcedony; of rich brown tone carved in deep relief to depict a sage wrapped in a long robe looking towards a horse, a pine branch overhead, serrated rockwork on the reverse; *height: 5.9cm*.

Suzhou School; 1730-1830

PROVENANCE: Colonel Kedzior
Sotheby's London, April 28th 1987, lot 700

The front of this bottle exhibits further characteristic features of this School. The carved details are in deep relief and yet are well rounded, to give a three dimensional effect. In addition, the principal scene appears to be slightly recessed and is framed by the minor details such as rockwork and trees.

Once again, the carver has succeeded in adding life to this scene, particularly in the swish of the horse's tail and the alert manner in which it has turned its head.

152

Rock crystal; colourless, suffused overall with minute green droplets, the front carved in low relief with a branch in blossom springing from a serrated rock cliff, the reverse with an inscription carved in low relief, *to cultivate prunus blossoms with a hoe, under the bright moon*, flanked by an incised seal, *lucid trinket*; *height: 6cm*.

Suzhou School; 1750-1830

PROVENANCE: Hugh Moss
Emily Byrne Curtis

EXHIBITED: Newark Museum, New Jersey, October/November 1982

At first glance this bottle has none of the characteristics of the Suzhou School which one expects. It is made of an unusual variety of rock crystal and not the usual materials, chalcedony or jade. It is of flattened rectangular form rather than rounded, and it possesses almost nothing in the way of interpreted inclusions.

Nevertheless, a close examination of this bottle leads one direct to the work of the Suzhou School. One other crystal bottle is known, which exhibits all the more usual characteristics[1], so that the material itself is not impossible. The branch is impeccably carved in low relief with outlines closely related to that of the pine tree on no. 149 above. There is one tiny whitish inclusion in the stone which has been encapsulated as a bud and the branch itself springs from serrated rockwork. Such subtle use of the material available is a classic Suzhou School touch and one can see in this the development from the style of the great Ming carver, Lu Zigang, which the Suzhou School represented. The relief inscription on the reverse is in a style found on several Suzhou examples (see no. 147 above) and there is an overall control of these elements which is rarely found on bottles from other workshops.

This particular bottle emphasizes the danger in being bound too rigidly by narrow rules in the analysis of art. Whilst rules and characteristics are of importance in building up a general foundation of knowledge, there will always be examples which appear to break many of the basic rules and yet on closer examination are indeed following them, but in an inspired and original way.

1. H. Moss. *Chinese Snuff Bottles of the Silica or Quartz Group*. p. 66, no. 173.

153

153

Chalcedony; of brownish tone with darker inclusions on front carved to depict a sage seated painting a rock from which dangle some cash, a smaller figure pouring a winepot, an incised inscription to one side, the reverse with a single gnarled pine beneath swirling rockwork; *height: 6.2cm.*

Suzhou School; 1750-1830

    PROVENANCE: Hugh Moss

    PUBLISHED: H. Moss. *Snuff Bottles of the Silica or Quartz Group*, p. 65, fig. 168

The inscription may be read: 'trying to think of a new way to make money every day', an apt phrase to apply to a bottle which was sold in 1961 to Hugh Moss for £4 and which he kept for twenty-five years.

154

Chalcedony; of pale greyish tone carved on front with a boy kneeling to present a bowl of fruit to two figures playing *weiqi*, the reverse with a figure in a sampan, a second figure peering out from behind serrated rockwork; *height: 6.2cm.*

Suzhou School; 1800-1880

    PROVENANCE: Honor Smith
                      The Belfort Collection

    EXHIBITED: Arcade Chaumet, Paris, June 1982, *Catalogue* no. 164

    PUBLISHED: H. Moss. *Snuff Bottles of the Silica or Quartz Group*, p. 62, fig. 163
                              V Jutheau. *Tabatières Chinoises*, p. 106, no. 4
                              Journal of the I.C.S.B.S., March 1979

A classic example of the Suzhou School, with the subjects framed by extensive swirling serrated rockwork. Once again, every nuance of colour has been used, with particular skill, in the case of the sampan, where the hull is subtly highlighted. The subjects are raised on a slightly inclined plateau, another device common to many Suzhou bottles to give the design greater depth. The treatment of the pine needles, however, with their simple incised needles, and the angular nature of the figures, suggests a nineteenth century date of manufacture.

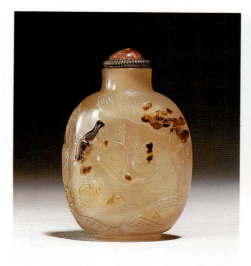
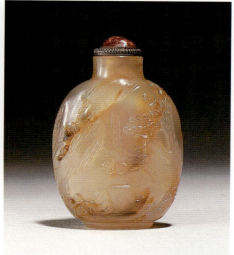

154

155

155

Chalcedony; dark honey colour with a white inclusion on one side carved to depict Liu Hai trailing a string of cash to tempt the three-legged toad, the beast on the reverse, exhaling a cloud of vapour, a gnarled tree on the shoulders; *height: 4.2cm.*

Suzhou School; 1800-1880

    PROVENANCE: Hugh Moss

    PUBLISHED: Hugh Moss. *Snuff Bottles of the Silica or Quartz Group*, p. 67, fig. 174

It is not known precisely how long the Suzhou School was in operation. Jade examples appear to provide the earliest examples, but the range of the chalcedony bottles nos. 147-151 above could very well have been carved in the eighteenth century. The fluidity of their designs and the control of the medium both compare well with other small carved objects such as brushpots, brushwashers and pendants which are accepted as of that period.

This particular bottle could have been carved a little later. Whilst the white inclusion has been brilliantly used, it represents a step away from the more simple patterns. Quality of carving is no longer sufficient and the addition of more colours is necessary to evoke the required response. This is typically a trend in most art forms as time passes and the patrons become bored with the original forms.

156

Chalcedony; of grey tone with natural inclusions in front, suggestive of a bat swooping towards a seated couple, clusters of rock on the reverse; *height: 5.2cm*.

1750-1860

PROVENANCE: Dr. Paula Hallett
Sotheby's, New York, 2nd December 1985, lot 78

A distinctive group of bottles exists, called 'silhouette chalcedony', by Moss[1]. These bottles rely on the skill of the lapidary in selecting a piece of stone and cutting it in such a way that any natural inclusions in the stone suggest a design. Usually a small amount of low relief carving is needed to bring the design to fruition, but in very rare examples, such as this one, a complete design can be released from the material solely by the skill in the cutting, without the need for any additional carving. Such bottles are amongst the most brilliant of all the various chalcedony types, and are still underrated by collectors.

A bottle such as this would have been greatly admired by the members of the literati who flourished during the first half of the nineteenth century, particularly the reverse, where the scene depicted by the various inclusions is open to many different interpretations.

1. H. Moss. *Chinese Snuff Bottles of the Silica or Quartz Group*, p. 36.

157   158

157

Chalcedony; dendritic; the front flattened to reveal a dense mass of fern-like inclusions; *height: 5.9cm*.

1750-1850

    PROVENANCE: Hugh Moss
                        The Belfort Collection

    EXHIBITED: Hong Kong Museum of Art, October 1978

    PUBLISHED: Hong Kong Museum. *Catalogue*, no. 198

This type of chalcedony is sometimes known as mocha stone. The markings, which are unusually well dispersed in this example, are caused by inclusions of manganese dioxide, and here resemble nine fish.

158

Chalcedony; of reddish-brown tone with natural uncarved inclusions in the stone depicting a duck pecking at a hanging morsel, a second duck to one side; *height: 6.7cm*.

1750-1860

    PROVENANCE: Gerd Lester

Another example of a design achieved without the need for any additional carving. It is worth noting the skill with which the first duck's eye has been pin-pointed and its tail-feathers suggested. Its neck appears to be craning to reach the morsel suspended just out of its reach. The second duck is pecking at a cluster of black seeds.

159

160

159

Chalcedony; beige with dark brown inclusions, lightly carved to depict a hatted figure, a fruiting branch draped over one shoulder, riding a camel, a dog yapping at its heals; *height: 6.7cm*.

1750-1860

PROVENANCE:	Hugh Moss
	The Belfort Collection
EXHIBITED:	Hong Kong Museum of Art, October 1978
PUBLISHED:	Hong Kong Museum. *Catalogue*, no. 202

An unusually sophisticated example of a silhouette agate with a complex and lively design brilliantly achieved. The paler muzzle of the camel is particularly inspired.

160

Chalcedony; of reddish brown tone with a darker inclusion on front lightly carved to depict a dog and incised with the inscription, *may the five blessings come to your door; height: 6.2cm*.

1800-1860

PROVENANCE: Gerd Lester

A further example of the lively design that should be looked for in the best of the 'Silhouette Group'.

The bat in China is the emblem of longevity and happiness and has none of the sinister overtones given to it in Western mythology. The design depicts the five blessings; old age, wealth, health, love of virtue and a natural death. This is owing to the similarity in the sound of the characters for 'bat' and 'happiness', both pronounced *fu*.

A number of bottles exist, closely related in style to this one, slightly more rectangular in form than numbers 158 and 159 above. One of these[1] depicts a European sailor holding a nautical instrument and might have been inspired by the presence of British sailors in Guangzhou in the 1830's and 1840's. It therefore seems likely that this sub-group might date from that period.

1. In the Collection of Mr. and Mrs. A.R. Kleiner.

161

162

161

Chalcedony; the greyish-brown stone with a dark inclusion on front, slightly carved to depict a waddling drake; *height: 6cm.*

1750-1860

PROVENANCE: Gerd Lester

A very good example of a silhouette chalcedony, where the slight amount of carving on the head has resulted in a very realistic depiction of a drake. The stone has a metallic tint and has been well hollowed out, a vital requirement in this type of bottle where the design is much enhanced by the ability of light to filter through the walls.

162

Chalcedony; of pale greyish tone with darker inclusions on front lightly carved to depict the He He Twins dancing with sprays of lotus; *height: 5.9cm.*

1800-1860

PROVENANCE: Gerd Lester

The He He are heavenly twins, usually portrayed holding a lotus and an opened box from which clouds emanate. They are a symbol of concord and harmony between married couples.

163

163

Chalcedony; of greyish tone with a russet inclusion on front lightly carved to reveal a fish jumping on its back out of water; *height: 6.2cm.*

1800-1860

It is unusual to find a silhouette chalcedony bottle with a russet skin. In this case, the carver has made skilful use of the variations of colour in the stone to suggest the gleaming scales of the fish.

164

Chalcedony; of pale grey tone, carved in low relief on front with a monkey, a fruiting peach bough over one shoulder, walking along a tree boat riding the waves, a bat swooping through the clouds on the reverse; *height: 5.9cm.*

1780-1860

    PROVENANCE: Hugh Moss
                        Alice B. McReynolds
                        Sotheby's New York, 16th April 1985, lot 109

This bottle provides a link between the preceding group of silhouette chalcedony bottles and a group of bottles carved in high relief in cameo style. The former group relies on a cutting away of excess material to reveal a design already almost apparent from the natural markings in the stone, whereas the cameo group relies on carving these natural inclusions in high relief.

In this case, brilliant use has been made of the natural inclusions in the stone, without any carving, to depict the boat and clouds, whilst the monkey, the waves and the bat have been detailed in low relief.

The monkey god, Sun Wukong, is reputed to have broken into the garden of the Queen of the Western Heavens, Xiwangmu, and stolen the peaches of immortality for himself.

164

165

165

Chalcedony; carved in rounded relief on front with an eagle attacking a lion, rocks to one side, the animal's mouth with an inlaid coral tongue, the reverse with a bee hovering above prunus; *height: 5.8cm.*

1800-1860

PROVENANCE: Gerd Lester

A classic example of the cameo style with its rounded relief carving, this bottle is unusual in having inlaid decoration added to enhance the design. The bee on the reverse is stylistically similar in carving to that of the monkey and bat of number 164 above.

166

166

Chalcedony; carved using the natural inclusions in the stone to depict an eagle perched on a rock flanked by a pine tree, the reverse with the crescent moon in relief above the incised inscription *Xingyouheng tang* (the Hall of Constancy); *height: 6.3cm.*

1810-1854

> PROVENANCE: Eric Young
> Sotheby's London, 3rd March 1987, lot 86

> PUBLISHED: Paul Moss. *Documentary Chinese Works of Art in Scholars' Taste*, p.170, no. 111

This bottle, like the earlier examples made for the fifth Prince Ding[1], is superbly worked. The carving, although bearing no similarities to that of the Suzhou School, has made use of every natural colour tone in the material to highlight the design and the hall mark itself is inscribed in impeccable *lishou* script.

Another bottle[2], although unmarked, is stylistically so similar to this example that it is safe to assume that they were both made by the same individual. It may eventually be possible to assign various of the cameo bottles, which are not obviously of the Suzhou School, to other workshops on the basis of such similarities.

The eagle is a symbol of strength and a picture of an eagle perched in a pine tree is a suitable gift for an old man, wishing him strength and long life.

1. See numbers 33 and 141 above.
2. Now in the Collection of Mr. and Mrs. James Li, previously sold at Sotheby's London, 20th April 1982, lot. 133.

167

Agate; of pebble form with a pine tree on front using green inclusions in the stone to depict the pine needles, five cranes hidden amongst the branches, each with eyes picked out; *height: 6.2cm.*

1800-1880

> PROVENANCE: Dr. Paula Hallett

The skill of the carver in this instance has been to use the differing layers of colour in the material to present a three-dimensional picture. The use of green to depict the pine needles is a clever device, but the success with which the eyes of each of the cranes has been highlighted using a natural inclusion in the stone shows a remarkable understanding of the medium.

167

168

168

Chalcedony; carved with a white recumbent duck looking up at various water-fowl in flight above aquatic fronds, the reverse with a pair of crested ducks beneath serrated rockwork; *height: 5.8cm.*

1780-1860

PROVENANCE: Hugh Moss

EXHIBITED: Hong Kong Museum of Art, October 1978

PUBLISHED: H. Moss. *Snuff Bottles of the Silica or Quartz Group*, p. 56, No. 146
Hong Kong Museum of Art. *Catalogue*, no. 214

Although this bottle possesses serrated rockwork it does not belong to the Suzhou school. The inclusions are well used, but more loosely than would be expected in a Suzhou example and the composition lacks the coherence one finds with the earlier school. Nevertheless this bottle does have features in common with a small group called 'eyeball' bottles by Moss[1]. The main feature of this group is demonstrated on the reverse where the eyes of the ducks are picked out in brown and appear to be looking straight at the beholder, from whatever angle the bottle is placed. The other main feature is the slightly rounded nature of the bottles leading to a flattened base. It is possible that this group came from the same workshop as number 166.

1. H. Moss. *Snuff Bottles of the Silica or Quartz Group*, p. 56.

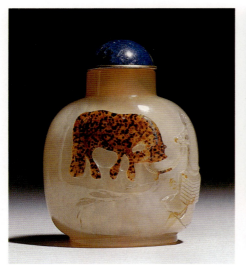

169

169

Chalcedony; the pale stone with a darker inclusion on front carved to depict a dappled tethered horse nuzzling at one of its legs, three butterflies on the reverse; *height: 6.2cm.*

1750-1860

> PROVENANCE: Hugh Moss
> Joan Wasserman
> The Belfort Collection
>
> EXHIBITED: Hong Kong Museum of Art, October 1978
>
> PUBLISHED: H. Moss. *Snuff Bottles of the Silica or Quartz Group*, p. 50, fig. 125
> Hong Kong Museum. *Catalogue*, no. 209
> V. Jutheau. *Tabatières Chinoises*, p. 98

In this example the carver has made brilliant use of the natural spotted markings in the stone to depict a dappled horse.

The subject matter of this bottle evokes the phrase *Ma dao gong song* ('the horse has arrived at the post'). This suggests unrealised potential and thus expresses a wish for speedy success for an undiscovered talent which is about to be put to the test[1].

1. Victor Graham. *Journal* of the I.C.S.B.S., Summer 1984, p. 15.

170

Chalcedony; carved in high relief, using dark inclusions in the stone, to depict two fisherman seated beneath clusters of lotus, a monkey holding a peach on the reverse; *height: 6cm.*

1800-1880

> PROVENANCE: Michael Stern
> Hugh Moss
>
> PUBLISHED: Sydney L. Moss. An Exhibition of Chinese Snuff Bottles, 1965, *Catalogue*, no. 47

The carving of this bottles relates closely in style to that of a bottle illustrated by Moss[1] and the monkey on the reverse can be compared to those on the front of no. 173 below in the angularity of its style.

1. H. Moss. *Snuff Bottles of the Silica or Quartz Group*, p. 55, no. 140.

170

171

171

Carnelian; various shades of red carved as two intertwined carp, their scales incised; *height: 5.3cm*.

1750-1880

PROVENANCE: Alex S. Cussons
Hugh Moss
Dr. Paula Hallett
Sotheby's, New York, 2nd December, 1986, lot 82

EXHIBITED: Hong Kong Museum of Art, October 1978

PUBLISHED: H. Moss. *Snuff Bottles of the Silica or Quartz Group*, p. 83, no. 214
Hong Kong Museum. *Catalogue*, no. 196

One of a small group of fish-subject bottles which might emanate from the same workshop.

The Chinese words for 'carp' and 'advantage' (li) are phonetically identical, so the carp symbolises a wish for benefit or advantage in business. It is also said that this fish on its journey upstream can jump the rapids on the Upper Yellow River. This feat is compared to success in the state examinations.

172   173

172

Chalcedony; carved in deep relief with a prancing tethered horse, using a white inclusion on a slightly speckled background; *height: 5.7cm.*

1750-1860

    PROVENANCE: Cyril Green
                        J. Haines
                        Hugh Moss
                        Dr. Paula Hallett

    EXHIBITED: Hong Kong Museum of Art, October 1978

    PUBLISHED: H. Moss. *Chinese Snuff Bottles*, No. 2, p. 24. pl.v
                        H. Moss. *Snuff Bottles of the Silica or Quartz Group*, p. 50, fig. 126
                        Hong Kong Museum. *Catalogue*, no. 211

It is rare to find a chalcedony bottle with a white skin. The colour emphasises the complete control over the carving, a factor which should always be looked for in judging any bottle of this group.

173

Chalcedony; carved in flattened relief with a monkey resting on its head, looking towards two other monkeys, the scene framed by serrated rockwork and the inscription *yan yuanbi*; *height: 5.9cm.*

1800-1880

    PROVENANCE: Christies South Kensington, 19th December, 1986, lot 8

A further example with serrated rockwork and yet not of the Suzhou School. The flatness of the relief carving is similar to that found on no. 170 above, but it is of a style which is not found in the Suzhou School.

Various Hardstones

174

Turquoise; of flattened form with a slightly flared neck, the front neatly incised with a Qianlong Imperial poem, the countersunk base inscribed in seal characters *Qianlong nianzhi* (*made in the Qianlong period*); *height: 5cm.*

Attributed to the Beijing Palace Workshops; 1736-1795

PROVENANCE: Alice B. McReynolds
Sotheby's New York, 16th April 1985, lot 135

PUBLISHED: *Journal* of the I.C.S.B.S., September 1977, p. 13, fig. 11

The neatness of the reign mark on this bottle compares well with that of the marks on the two jade bottles (numbers 24 and 25 above). The Qianlong Emperor inscribed many thousands of objects with his poems and whilst the practice continued after his death there is no reason to doubt the authenticity of this example. The small size of the bottle, the quality of the calligraphy and the extent of the patination on the surface all point to an eighteenth century date of manufacture[1].

Turquoise is a relatively porous material and it changes to a greenish tone after prolonged contact with the oils of the human hand.

1. Compare with the inscribed imperial yellow glass bottle, no. 132 below.

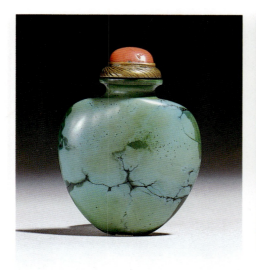

175

Turquoise; of flattened spade shape with a wide flared neck, the stone of mottled turquoise and green tone; *height: 5.1cm*.

1750-1820

PROVENANCE:	Bob C. Stevens
	Sotheby's Honolulu, 7th November 1981, lot 154
	The Belfort Collection
EXHIBITED:	Mikimoto Hall, Tokyo, *Catalogue*, No. 245
	Arcade Chaumet, Paris, June 1982, *Catalogue*, no. 221
PUBLISHED:	Bob C. Stevens. *The Collector's Book of Snuff Bottles*, no. 601
	Hugh Moss. *Chinese Snuff Bottles*, No. 4, col.pl.G
	Journal of the I.C.S.B.S., September 1977, p. 11, no. 4

The patination on this bottle is exactly where it should be; on the centre, around the shoulders and around the mouth just the areas which would be exposed to the most handling. This together with the overall simplicity in style and the fairly poor quality of the stone point towards an eighteenth century date of manufacture.

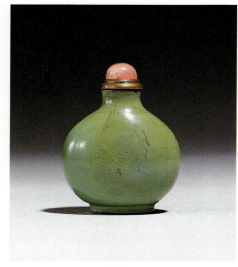

176

176

Turquoise; of rounded form supported on a neatly finished footrim, the material extensively patinated to an overall greenish tone; *height: 4.1cm.*

18th Century

> PROVENANCE: Hugh Moss
> Dr. Paula Hallett

This bottle is remarkably close in shape and size to the 18th century group which is enamelled on copper, discussed above.

177

Inkstone (*tuan* stone); dark greenish slate carved into ten gently fluted panels each enclosing stylised calligraphy including a dedication, *for the approval of his excellency, respected cousin Yuezhi* with the signature *engraved by Zhenzhi, height: 5.2cm.*

1770-1860

> PROVENANCE: Bob C. Stevens
> Sotheby's Honolulu, 7th November 1981, lot 183
> The Belfort Collection
>
> EXHIBITED: Mikimoto Hall, Tokyo, October 1978, *Catalogue*, no. 267
> Arcade Chaumet, *Catalogue*, no. 222
>
> PUBLISHED: Bob C. Stevens. *The Collector's Book of Snuff Bottles*, no. 660
> H. Moss. *Chinese Snuff Bottles*, No. 4, p. 39, no. 6

Tuan is the name given to the particular variety of slate which is best suited for the grinding of ink for use in painting or calligraphy. It is thus a material both familiar to and enjoyed by the literati.

This particular bottle with its narrow panels and meticulously executed raised borders is of outstanding elegance.

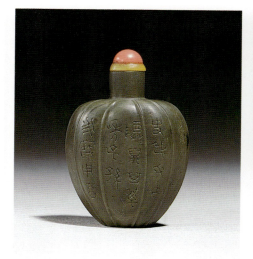

177

178

178

Turquoise; of natural pebble form carved as a fruiting melon enveloped by broad leaves and a gnarled stalk; *length: 5.9cm*.

1770-1820

PROVENANCE: Dr. Paula Hallett

This bottle compares closely in its shape and the style of its carving to the typical jade fruit carvings of the Qianlong period. A very similar bottle is in the Victoria and Albert Museum (ref.c. 1938-1910), from the Salting Bequest which was already in the Museum Collection by 1895.

Inkstone; of flattened rectangular form, incised on four sides with Wang Xizhi's *Lanting* Preface, the base incised with an inscription stating that the version of the Preface copied was that by the late Qing calligrapher Weng Tanqi and that it was inscribed on the bottle at the *Cho Zhai* (the Unsophisticated Studio) in the first summer month of 1890 of the Guangxu period; *height: 5.5cm.*

1890

PROVENANCE:	Alice Boney
	Hugh Moss
	Dr. Paula Hallett
EXHIBITED:	Hong Kong Museum of Art, October 1978
PUBLISHED:	Hong Kong Museum. *Catalogue,* no. 130
	Viviane Jutheau. *Tabatières Chinoises*, p. 119, fig. 3

The Lanting Gathering took place in A.D.353, when forty-two scholars were invited to the Orchid Pavilion (Lanting) near Shanyin, Zhejiang Province, for the Spring Purification Festival. A competition took place which involved the composition of a poem and Wang Xizhi, generally regarded as the greatest of all calligraphers, composed the passage of 324 characters known as the Lanting Preface, whilst under the influence of alcohol. He considered it his masterpiece and to this day it is regarded as the finest example of running script ever produced. Although the original has long since been lost numerous copies were made throughout the following centuries[1].

Extracts from the Preface may be found on numbers 251 and 288 below.

1. G. Tsang and H. Moss. *Arts From the Scholar's Studio*, no. 28.

180

Malachite: of ovoid form, the mottled material smoothly patinated; *height: 5.6cm.*

1780-1860

    PROVENANCE: The Belfort Collection

    PUBLISHED: V Jutheau. *Tabatières Chinoises*, p. 119, fig.1

Although malachite was available in China throughout the snuff bottle period it is rare to find an example of any great age. The patination and degree of wéar and tear on this bottle, together with the shape and simple design, point to a relatively early date of manufacture.

181

Sapphire matrix; of rounded form, the mottled opaque blue material suffused with chatoyancy; *height: 5.5cm.*

1800-1860

    PROVENANCE: The Belfort Collection

    PUBLISHED: V. Jutheau. *Tabatières Chinoises*, p. 116, fig. 3

Sapphire matrix is not pure enough to provide stones of gem quality, but when ground into powder it was used by jade carvers as an abrasive. It is very rare to find a snuff bottle in this material.

182

Jet; of circular section and slender ovoid form, supported on a neatly finished footrim; *height: 6.6cm.*

1820-1880

Jet is a compact material which is fossilised carbonised wood. It is relatively soft, with a hardness of 4 on the Moh's scale and it is rarely found in the form of a Snuff Bottle. Jet is a symbol of double longevity.

180

181

182

Organic
Materials

183

Coral; of flattened form carved overall with squirrels clambering amongst fruiting grape vines, the foot carved and pierced with the gnarled trunk to form the base; *height: 6.2cm*.

1730-1800

PROVENANCE: Bob C Stevens
                        Sotheby's Honolulu, 7th November 1981, lot 149
                        The Belfort Collection

EXHIBITED: Hong Kong Museum of Art, September 1977, *Catalogue*, no. 255
                        Mikimoto Hall, Tokyo, October 1978, *Catalogue*, no 235
                        Arcade Chaumet, Paris, June 1982, *Catalogue*, no. 223

PUBLISHED: Bob C. Stevens. *The Collector's Book of Snuff Bottles*, no. 1019
                        H. Moss. *Chinese Snuff Bottles*, No. 4, p. 37, col. pl. D

Coral is a calcerous deposit of marine polyps. It was available to the Chinese as early as the Han Dynasty and was regarded as a symbol of longevity.

The overall control of the design of this bottle is very good and the pattern is not dissimilar in feeling to a magnificent coral box and cover in the Beijing Palace Museum which was sent as a tribute to the Court, from Guangzhou during the Yongzheng reign (1723-1735).[1]

1. Yang Boda. *Tributes From Guangdong to the Qing Court*, p. 35, fig. 9.

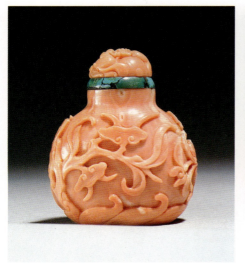

184

184

Coral; carved in graduated relief with a bat suspending a tasselled *swastika* lozenge, the reverse with lotus and *lingzhi* fungus, crested waves around the base; *height: 4.3cm.*

Qianlong period, 1736-1795

> PROVENANCE: Hugh Moss
> Dr. Paula Hallett
>
> EXHIBITED: Hong Kong Museum of Art, October 1978
>
> PUBLISHED: Hong Kong Museum. *Catalogue*, no. 123

The quality of the graduated relief carving and the superb control demonstrated by the artist in his use of the space available are both comparable to the best Qianlong jade carving. The use of wax plugs to fill gaps in the material was also a device used in the eighteenth century, when supplies of large pieces of coral were limited, and this technique is apparent on the bottle.

The lozenge was one of the *babao* (Eight Precious Objects). The *swastika* is one of the oldest symbols in China and was used as both a symbol of good luck and an emblem of immortality.

185

Coral; of flattened form carved overall with nine bats swooping amongst clouds; *height: 7.3cm.*

1750-1820

Bottles with very similar vigorous carving are illustrated by Bob Stevens, *The Collector's Book of Snuff Bottles*, no. 604, and in the Hong Kong Museum, *Catalogue*, October 1978, no. 124.

Nine is the ultimate male number in Chinese mythology being the square of three, itself a male number.

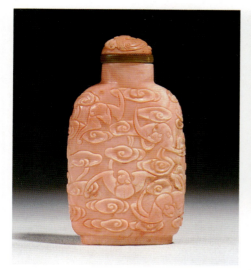

185

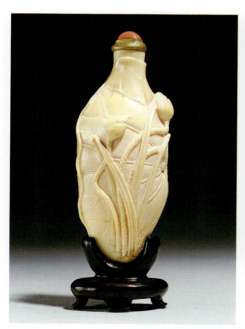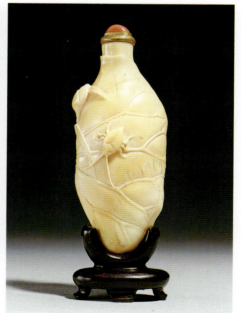

186

186

Ivory; carved in the form of a curled lotus leaf, the stalk extending up one side, a beetle resting on the reverse; *height: 8.3cm.*

1840-1880

PROVENANCE: Dr. Paula Hallett
Sotheby's New York, 2nd December, 1985, lot 66

This bottle was probably the inspiration for the porcelain bottle of almost identical form, number 240 below.

187

Ivory; carved as two carp standing face to face, their mouth joined to form the opening at the top, crested waves lapping the base extending up the sides, the eyes inlaid in black, the base incised with the four character seal mark *Qianlong nianzhi* (*made in the Qianlong period*); *height: 7.5cm.*

Beijing Palace Workshops; 1736-1795

PROVENANCE: The Krolik Collection
Hugh Moss
Robert Hall

EXHIBITED: Hong Kong Museum of Art, October, 1978

PUBLISHED: Hong Kong Museum. *Catalogue*, no. 32
V. Jutheau. *Tabatières Chinoises*, p. 128, fig. 4
Journal of the I.C.S.B.S., December 1975, p. 13 and December 1977, p. 28

This bottle forms one of a very rare group of which less than thirty specimens have been recorded. Whilst there is no documentary evidence that these bottles were made in the Palace Workshops, the circumstantial evidence is strong.

Each of the bottles bears a Qianlong reign mark, either in a seal or in running script. Two bottles are known with a Jiaqing reign mark[1]. They all appear to be made from a similar stock of ivory and have the patination, wear and tear and discolouration which one would expect from an ivory piece dating from the eighteenth century. Indeed, in this respect they compare well with other documented ivory carvings[2].

They are almost uniformly well carved with the flow in design and control of the space available which characterises most carvings of the eighteenth century and which was rarely repeated successfully by later imitations.

Finally, there is a well documented group of porcelain snuff bottles, clearly later modelled from moulds of the ivory bottles, which date from the Jiaqing reign. The exact porcelain counterpart of the twin fish bottle illustrated is in the Chester Beattie Collection in Dublin and entered that Collection around 1880.

The above factors, together with the close similarity in style of the Jiaqing example referred to above, point to a date of manufacture for the group during the second half of the eighteenth century.

Once the authenticity of the group is established the question of their place of manufacture can be addressed. The seal marks provide the main pointer towards a Palace Workshop origin. These are invariably written in four characters and when in seal script, as in this example, they compare very closely with the seal marks on other small items of undoubted Palace origin, such as the enamelled glass snuff bottle, number 15 above.

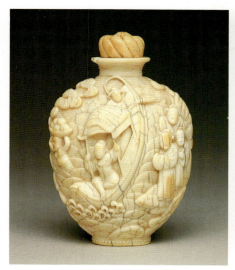

Where small works of art, produced at other centres, possess reign marks written in seal characters these contain usually six characters, rather than the four which was a characteristic of Palace work.

The group, as a whole, possesses such coherence in style that it must have been the work of two or three carvers at the most. The wares of such a small workshop, if it existed outside the Palace, would have been unlikely to have found their way to the Palace, and that they were intended for Palace use is shown by the fact that they are marked.

1. One, in the Burghley House Collection, is illustrated by H. Moss. *Chinese Snuff Bottles*, No. 6, p. 5, fig. 0.5.
2. O.C.S. London. *Chinese Ivories from the Shang to the Qing*.

188

Ivory; carved with a continuous scene depicting a voluptuous lady seated in a boat, watched by the Eight Immortals standing on clouds, the scene all on a ground of incised waves, the base incised with the four character mark *Qianlong nianzhi (made in the Qianlong period); height: 6.3cm.*

Beijing Palace Workshops; 1736-1795

    PROVENANCE: Lydia Tovey
                          Sotheby's 28th April, 1987 lot 652

This bottle is carved in the rounded sculptural style characteristic of the group as a whole. The patination, crackle in the material and quality of the carving are all entirely consistent with its dating towards the latter half of the eighteenth century.

The reign mark in this case is thinly incised in four characters within a double square. Indeed, the bottles of this entire group can be divided into two sub-groups, those which possess formal seal marks and those which posses these thinly incised character marks and this might be a basis for distinguishing the work of two different artists.

As a general observation, those bottles in the rounded relief style all appear to have the incised character marks, whereas those which appear to have more individuality in style, such as the fish bottle, number 187 above, the spade-shaped bottle, number 190 below, and a bottle in the form of a duck[1], now in the Collection of the Hong Kong Museum of Art, each possess the seal mark.

1. Exhibited at the Hong Kong Museum of Art, October, 1978, *Catalogue*, no. 33.

189

Ivory; carved on each side with a boat full of figures riding on a rough sea of crested waves, the base encircled by lotus and the shoulders with cloud scrolls beneath a petal collar, the base incised with the four character mark *Qianlong nianzhi* (*made in the Qianlong period*); *height: 6.9cm*.

Beijing Palace Workshops; 1736-1795

    PROVENANCE: Frederick Knight
                       Sotheby's London, 9th June, 1981, lot 60
                       Dr. Paula Hallett

This bottle bears the distinctive incised four character mark within a double square, thereby linking it with number 188 above.

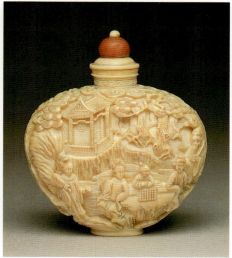

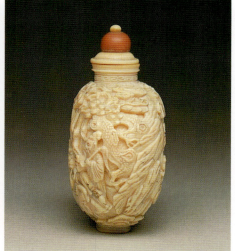

190

Ivory; carved in deep relief with a lady and baby riding a water-buffalo, attended by a figure holding a banner, the reverse with figures seated playing *weiqi* in front of a pavilion in a pine wood, the base incised with the four character seal mark *Qianlong nianzhi* (*made in the Qianlong period*); *height: 5.4cm.*

Beijing Palace Workshops; 1736-1795

   PROVENANCE: Sotheby's London, 28th April 1987, lot 697

Although this bottle is substantially different in style to most of the examples of this group it is linked by the neatly incised seal mark, the etched details on the rockwork and the treatment of the neck and undoubtedly belongs to the group, although possibly by a different artist.

The treatment of the pine tree and needles and the overall disposition of the subject matter compare closely to that found on contemporary cinnabar lacquer carvings.

191

Ivory; carved on each side with figures in a boat surrounded by lotus leaves, a bearded sage standing beneath a canopy on one shoulder, the base incised with the four character seal mark *Qianlong nianzhi* (*made in the Qianlong period*); *height: 5.5cm*.

Beijing Palace Workshops; 1736-1795

    PROVENANCE: Lydia Tovey
                       Sotheby's London, 28th April 1987, lot 653

This bottle is slightly unusual in style in that the relief detail is flattened. In keeping with the other bottles of this group which have unusual features it bears an incised seal mark similar to that of numbers 187 and 190.

192

Ivory; carved as the figure of Liu Hai, his cloak open at the chest to reveal a necklace of cash; *height: 8cm.*

1750-1820

The well sculpted rounded features, carefully finished hands and neatly incised hair on this figure all compare well with such features on eighteenth century ivory carved figures. The stopper has skilfully been disguised as the top-knot and this, together with the small size of the figure are pointers to its having been made originally as a snuff bottle and not as a figure which was later converted.

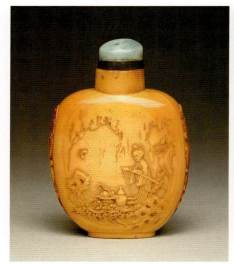  

193

Hornbill; carved in low relief on front with the Immortal, Lan Caihe steering a tree boat, the reverse with an archaic bronze inscription signed with the seals *Bai Shi*, the shoulders with the red sheath carved as a dragon; *height: 5.8cm.*

Daoguang period, circa 1835-1850

PROVENANCE: The Ko Collection

Hornhill is the ivory material obtained from the casque of the hornbill, *Rhinoplax vigil* which is found only on the islands of the Malaysian archipelago and in particular, in Borneo. The bird is extremely difficult to capture and there is documentary evidence that hornbill ivory was regarded as of great value and rarety in China from at least Song times (the Song Dynasty ruled from 960 A.D. until 1278 A.D.)[1]

A handfull of bottles have been recorded, signed by this artist. One, formerly in the Edward Dwyer Collection[2], bears the date and inscription Daoguang period 1843, and another, the date 1836 (Exhibited at the Hong Kong Museum of Art, October 1978, *Catalogue* no. 147). Each of the bottles by this artist is superbly carved in low graduated relief with minutely detailed figures and contains a fine network of crackles around the neck. The red skin of the sheath has been incorporated into the design on the shoulders.

1. T. Harrison. 'Ho-tung Hornbill Ivory', *Chinese Snuff Bottles*, No. 5, p. 82.
2. H. Moss. *Chinese Snuff Bottles*, No. 5, p. 92.

194

Hornbill; carved in low relief on each side with a circular panel enclosing a boy leaping beneath a pine tree, the red skin on the shoulders carved with a dragon; *height: 6.3cm*.

1830-1850

PROVENANCE: Alex Cussons
                       Hugh Moss
                       The Belfort Collection

EXHIBITED: Arcade Chaumet, Paris, June 1982, *Catalogue*, no. 225

PUBLISHED: H. Moss. *Chinese Snuff Bottles*, No. 5, p. 96, figs. 20-22
                     V. Jutheau. *Tabatières Chinoises*, p. 124, figs. 1 and 2
                     Journal of the I.C.S.B.S., December 1976 and March 1979

Although this bottle is carved by a different artist to the previous example, it is so similar in its patination, its wear and the network of crackles around the neck that it is likely to date from approximately the same period.

195

195

Hornbill; of flattened form carved on front with a recessed panel enclosing a stork swooping down towards a pine tree and two further storks on the ground, the reverse with a lengthy inscription; *height: 7.5cm.*

1830-1850

PROVENANCE: Gerd Lester

Another bottle related in style to the preceding example, although with slightly more angular carving.

196

Cinnabar lacquer; carved on one side with an elaborately dressed court figure bowing to a lady in a landscape, the reverse depicting Fu hiding in a tree spying down on Qiaoniang seated in a garden; *height: 6.4cm.*

Qianlong period, 1736-1795

PROVENANCE: The Belfort Collection

EXHIBITED: Arcade Chaumet, Paris, June 1982, *Catalogue*, no. 230

Lacquer is derived from the sap of the lacquer tree, (*rhus vernicifera*). The sap is drained through an incision in the bark, collected and then applied in layers to the surface to be decorated. The art of lacquer work has been known in China since at least the Han period (206 BC to 220 AD) and it particularly flourished during the Ming and Qing Dynasties[1].

The colour of cinnabar lacquer is obtained by mixing cinnabar (mercury) with the lacquer sap. An object such as this bottle would have required the application of at least one hundred and fifty coats of lacquer, each layer being allowed to dry before the application of the following layer. The completed shell was then carved down towards the original surface.

Numerous lacquer items survive with the reign mark of the Qianlong Emperor[2] and they all exhibit a distinctive style of carving in deep rounded relief, similar to that on this bottle. The level of patination and wear is also what one would expect of a bottle of this age, with details worn down and the distinctive shine imparted by the oils of the hand.

The subject illustrated on this bottle, the story of Qiaoniang, is one of the collection assembled by Pu Songhing in 1679 under the title of *Liao Zhai ji yi*[3].

1. R. Soame Jenyns & W. Watson. *Chinese Art*, Vol. 2.
2. *Catalogue, of an Exhibition of Lacquer Wares in the National Palace Museum, Taiwan*, August, 1981.
3. V. Mead. *Journal*, of the I.C.S.B.S., September 1980, p. 25.

196

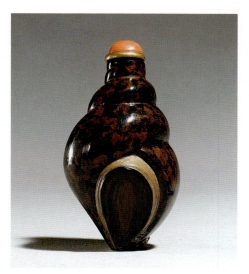

197

197

Lacquer; moulded silk in the form of a conch shell, painted in dark brown and gold-dappled lacquer; *height: 5.7cm.*

Fuzhou; 1800-1880

    PROVENANCE: Gerd Lester

Fuzhou was one of the main centres for the manufacture of lacquer wares in China and whilst there is no actual evidence that this bottle was made there, Fuzhou was particularly known for its lacquer products on a silk or other textile base[1].

1. V. Jutheau. *Journal* of the I.C.S.B.S., June 1981, p. 22 fig. 4.

198

198

Tangerine; moulded with a circular panel enclosing a spray of prunus springing from rockwork, the base with the cyclical date *kui wei* (1823 or 1883), the shoulders with double *shou* characters and the reverse inscribed with the name of the recipient (illegible), followed by *Xiang qiang yi shov shov zeng (fragrant pure substance will add years to your life, from Shou Zeng) height: 5.5cm.*

1823 or 1883

    PROVENANCE: Emily Byrne Curtis

    EXHIBITED: Newark Museum, New Jersey, October/November 1982

Tangerine skin, like gourd, becomes very hard and durable when drained of all its liquid content. This bottle with its apparent lack of sophistication and naturalness is in classic literati taste.

199

Bamboo veneer (*zhuhuang*); of hexagonal section and baluster form, carved in low relief on each side with archaic dragons, between moulded petals encircling the foot and shoulders; *height: 5.2cm.*

Qianlong period, 1736-1795

    PROVENANCE: The Meiling Collection
                        Sotheby's New York, 3rd March 1984, lot 126

    PUBLISHED: *Journal* of the I.C.S.B.S., Summer 1984

Zhuhuang, or 'bamboo's yellow', is the inner core of the bamboo. The best examples came from the provinces of Henan, Hebei and Sichuan, along the central and upper Yangtze Valley. The core is carved away leaving the thin layer of skin on top to form the design.

This technique was much in fashion in Court circles of the Qianlong period and several examples survive both in Taiwan and in the National Palace Museum, Beijing, which demonstrate a style of decoration and carving very close to that of this bottle[1].

1. Wango Weng & Yang Boda. *The Palace Museum*, *Peking*, p. 286, fig. 193.

199

200

200

Bamboo root; a double bottle carved following the natural form of the material to depict two pods enveloped by a gnarled stalk with broad leaves and trailing tendrils, inscribed on one side with an inscription and the signature *Zhuang Baopu of Jiading; length: 11cm.*

1750-1850

PROVENANCE: The Ko Collection

Jiading was a noted bamboo carving centre.

This bottle embodies many of the most cherished ideals of the literati. It is made from bamboo, a material closely linked to the literati from early times because of its elegance, the manner in which it grows, straight and true, and the difficulty in painting it as a subject[1]. It has also been skilfully carved so that it retains most of its natural shape, thereby realising that fusion between the works of man and nature which the literati regarded as one of the essences of art.

1. G. Tsang & H. Moss. *Arts From the Scholar's Studio*, No. 67.

201

Gourd; moulded to depict a continuous scene of a dog and two birds on a rockwork base, divided by chrysanthemums, bamboo and *lingzhi* fungus, the base moulded with the four character mark *Daoguang nianzhi* (*made in the Daoguang period*); *height: 4.2cm.*

Beijing Palace Workshops; Daoguang period, 1821-1850

PROVENANCE: Raymond Li
The Belfort Collection

EXHIBITED: Hong Kong Museum of Art 1977, *Catalogue*, no. 266
Arcade Chaumet, Paris, June 1982, *Catalogue*, no. 236

PUBLISHED: V. Jutheau. *Tabatières Chinoises*, p. 137, fig 5

The art of moulding gourds flourished during the eighteenth and first half of the nineteenth centuries. A number of bowls, brushpots, vases and cricket cages have survived, many of which bear Kangxi and Qianlong four character marks which rank very high in the hierarchy of imperial marks[1]. These marks usually contain the Emperor's reign name together with the characters *shangwan* (appreciated treasure) or *yuwan* (imperial treasure). A number of gourds also exist, made for the fifth Prince Ding, Zaichuan, with his personal hall mark, *Xingyouheng Tang*[2].

Such grand marks on a series of objects points not only to a direct Imperial interest but also to a probable place of manufacture within the Palace workshops[3].

Fewer Daoguang specimens exist but Tsang and Moss publish two examples of cricket cages thus marked.

This bottle would have been made in the primary mould system. The mould was first carved of wood, usually in several parts, and the gourd was then grown inside the mould so that its form was confined to the shape of the mould.

1. For an explanation of the hierarchy of marks see number 1 above.
2. The importance of the *Xingyouheng Tang* is explained number 141 above.
3. G. Tsang & H. Moss. 'Chinese Decorated Gourds', *Catalogue* of the International Asian Antiques Fair, 1983.

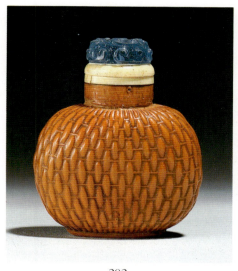 

202   203

202

Gourd; moulded overall with a wickerwork pattern, the mouth with an ivory collar; *height: 5.8cm*.

1800-1850

A very fine example of crisp moulding. One bottle with similar decoration in a private English Collection is known with the four character mark of Daoguang.

203

Amber; carved on each side with confronted archaistic dragons between a band of petal lappets encircling the shoulders; *height: 5.8cm*.

Attributed to the Beijing Palace Workshops; 1780-1860

    PROVENANCE: Hugh Moss
                      Dr. Paula Hallett

The treatment of the petal lappets, the *ruyi* heads and the archaistic dragons on this bottle relates very closely in style to that of the Palace glass bottles, numbers 66 and 67 above.

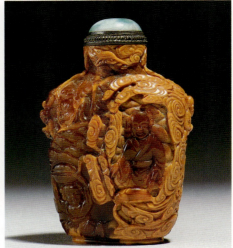

204

204

Root amber; carved overall with the Goddess, Xi Wangmu seated in a chariot holding a basket with the peaches of immortality, surrounded by the He He twins, Liu Hai and the three-legged toad, and Shou Lao, all surrounded by clouds; *height: 7.7cm.*

1882-1880

PROVENANCE: Hugh Moss
Dr. Paula Hallett
Sotheby's New York, 2nd December 1985, lot 70

EXHIBITED: Hong Kong Museum of Art, October 1978

PUBLISHED: Hong Kong Museum. *Catalogue*, no. 142

Root amber is the variety which contains inclusions of differing colour and opacity. The carver in this instance has made skillful use of the contrasting patches of clear and opaque material to highlight the subject-matter.

Xi Wangmu was the queen of the Western Heavens who resided in a park within the Kunlin mountains. She was the guardian of the peaches of immortality, later stolen by the monkey, Sun Wukong. By tradition she visited the Emperor on the 7th day of the 7th Month, (a feast-day devoted to Women).

205

Amber; a natural pebble carved as the figure of Liu Hai, a train of cash draped over his shoulders, the three-legged toad at his feet; *height: 6.7cm.*

1800-1880

PROVENANCE: Hugh Moss
Dr. Paula Hallett

Figural snuff bottles in any material are rare, but particularly so in amber.

205

206

206

Amber; a natural pebble carved overall with fruiting double-gourds, a gnarled stalk and leaves trailing tendrils; *height: 8cm.*

1750-1820

PROVENANCE: Gerd Lester

The style of carving and subject matter of this bottle compare closely to that found on eighteenth century jade pebble carvings. The quality of the finish on this bottle is unusually high for an amber bottle, with no rough patches on the polished surface.

207

207

Pearl; a Pair of bottles each constructed from several sections of natural encrusted pearls with metal mounted necks inlaid with tourmalines and garnets, beneath enamelled *shou* characters; *height: 6.1cm*.

1850-1900

    PROVENANCE: The Ko Collection

No other bottles of this type appear to be recorded, although others with just ornamental pearls are known. The decoration on the necks is typical of late nineteenth century court style and the rarity and value of the pearl material would tend to point towards a court destination.

208

Laque burgauté; in the form of a cicada, the black lacquer ground inlaid with geometric patterns in mother-of-pearl chips of differing colour; *height: 6.1cm*.

Japan; 1800-1880

    PROVENANCE: Bob C. Stevens
                         Sotheby's New York, 26th March 1982, lot 198
                         The Belfort Collection

    PUBLISHED: H. Moss. *Chinese Snuff Bottles*, No. 4, p. 37, col pl. E
                         Bob C. Stevens. *The Collector's Book of Snuff Bottles*, no. 1027

This technique of inlaying a design on a bed of lacquer, using chips of mother-of-pearl, was popular in China from the Tang Dynasty onwards. It appeared in Japan some time during the nineteenth century and was employed on a large group of snuff bottles many of which date from the twentieth century.

This particular bottle is probably Japanese. The minute gold speckled chips around the eyes are a specifically Japanese variation of the technique. Nevertheless, the piece has some considerable age because it exhibits a large degree of patination. It is of superb quality, with the geometric inlays, of unusual complexity, imitating the webbing of the wings.

208

209

209

Laque burgauté; of flattened form inlaid on one side with chrysanthemum and on the reverse with lilies, using mother-of-pearl in gold and differing shades of silver; *height: 6.9cm.*

Japan; 1840-1880

    PROVENANCE: Michael Stern
                      Sydney L. Moss Ltd

    PUBLISHED: Sydney Moss. *Catalogue*, of Chinese Snuff Bottles, 1965, no. 129
                      H. Moss. *Snuff Bottles of China*, no. 151 and cover

The treatment of the flowers on this bottle is characteristically Japanese in style with the rounded stylised blooms.

210

Coconut; of flattened form carved on each side with a slightly recessed panel enclosing an archaistic inscription, an inscription in conventional script on one shoulder; *height: 6.5cm.*

1800-1860

PROVENANCE: The Fulford Collection
H.G. Beasley
Mac Beasley
Sotheby's London, 2nd July 1984, lot 76

This bottle, made from a material of no value in itself, is typical of the type much admired by the literati class. This class exhibited almost an inverted snobbery in their distate for precious materials such as gold or jade and their liking for simple materials carved with inscriptions with scholarly allusions.

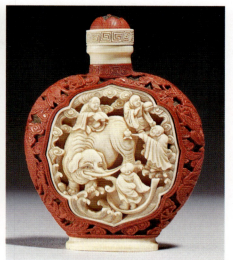

211

Lacquer with ivory panels; of large size, inlaid with a quatrefoil panel enclosing on one side four Immortals surrounding the Japanese God, Daruma and on the reverse with four more Immortals, one riding an elephant, the shoulders carved with cinnabar lacquer dragons on a brown wave ground, the base incised with a four character Qianlong mark; *height: 8.2cm*.

Japan; 1860-1920

PROVENANCE: Janus Szekeres
Sotheby's New York, 27th October 1986, lot 121

This bottle forms part of a small but very distinctive group of bottles. Less than ten have been recorded and they are almost certainly all by the same hand. They possess either ivory panels on a lacquer ground or lacquer panels on an ivory ground and they each have separately fitted necks with matching floral-shaped stoppers. They are uniformly superbly carved with vigour and neatly incised details and are possibly inspired by the Chinese Imperial Ivory School. They each possess an incised four character Qianlong mark on the base. The subject matter appears to be an amalgam of Chinese and Japanese legends and in this case the existance of the Japanese legendary figure, Daruma in his characteristic cowl, points conclusively to their Japanese origins.

Japanese carving of this quality flourished during the second half of the nineteenth century but after that date tended to become wooden and uninspired, and the extent of the patination and wear on these bottles is consistent with an age of around eighty to one hundred years.

212

Ivory with lacquer panels; carved on each side with a three-colour lacquer panel enclosing groups of females in a garden, inset into an ivory framework carved with dragons amongst clouds, the base incised with the four character mark of Qianlong; *height: 6.1cm*.

Japan; 1860-1920

PROVENANCE: Eric Hancock
Hugh Moss
The Belfort Collection

EXHIBITED: Arcade Chaumet, Paris, June 1982, *Catalogue* no. 229

PUBLISHED: H. Moss. *Chinese Snuff Bottles*, No. 2, p. 19, col. pl. D
V. Jutheau. *Tabatières Chinoises*, p. 132
Journal of the I.C.S.B.S., March 1979 and June 1981

213

Ivory with lacquer panels; carved on one side with a cinnabar lacquer panel on a black ground depicting Huang Chenyen riding through a landscape and on the reverse with a scholar seated in a pavilion nestled beneath towering cliffs, in black on a red ground, the panels inset into an ivory frame carved on one side with the Japanese Goddess Benten and on the opposite side with a boy riding a *Howo* bird, the base incised with a four character Qianlong mark; *height: 7.8cm.*

Japan; 1860-1920

    PROVENANCE: Sotheby's New York, 1st July 1985, lot 192

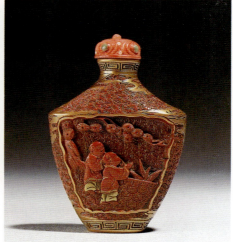

214

214

Cinnabar lacquer; carved in low relief on one side with an elaborately dressed lady seated by a table laden with a bowl of fruit, the reverse with two small boys clapping their hands, the shoulders decorated with a brocade diaper and gilded clouds; *height: 6cm.*

Japan; 1860-1920

This bottle is clearly related to the preceding group in the style of its carving. The flattened gilded clouds are a typically Japanese decorative device.

Very few of this group have been recorded. Two were illustrated by H. Moss, *Chinese Snuff Bottles*, No. 3, p. 43, figs. 44 and 46.

215

Ivory; carved and pierced in deep relief on one side with a phoenix perched on an ornamental rock looking up at two song birds perched within the dense foliage of flowering tree peonies, the reverse with an exotic crested bird perched on a prunus bough with chrysanthemum to one side, the base inscribed with a seal mark *Qianlong nianzhi*; *height: 6.1cm.*

Japan; 1860-1920

PROVENANCE: Cyril Green
Hugh Moss
The Belfort Collection

EXHIBITED: Arcade Chaumet, Paris, June 1982, *Catalogue*, no. 228

PUBLISHED: H. Moss. *Chinese Snuff Bottles*, no. 2, p. 20, col. pl. I
V. Jutheau. *Tabatières Chinoises*, p. 127

This bottle was believed for many years to be Chinese but the treatment of the phoenix and the stylised nature of the flowers are very distinctively Japanese in flavour. The shape of the bottle also compares closely with another group of Japanese ivory bottles, one of which was illustrated by Bob C. Stevens, *The Collector's Book of Snuff Bottles*, no. 775.

Nevertheless, the quality and control of the carving are outstanding and the question of whether the bottle is of Japanese or Chinese origin should play no part in its appreciation as a work of art.

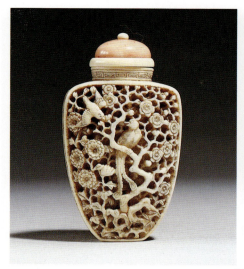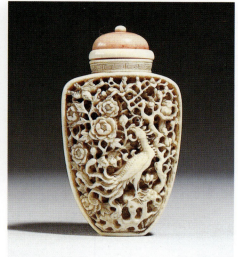

215

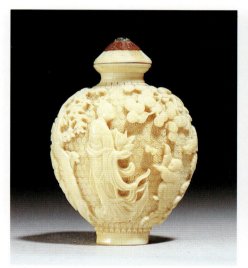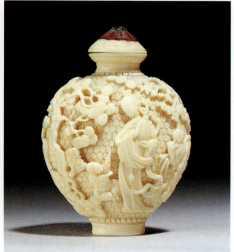

216

216

Ivory; of ovoid form carved in relief on each side with an elegantly dressed lady and a small boy, on a diaper ground framed by pine trees, a two character Qianlong mark incised on the base; *height: 6.5cm.*

Japan; 1860-1920

PROVENANCE: Sotheby's London, 28th October 1969, lot 67
Cyril Green
Hugh Moss
Emily Byrne Curtis

PUBLISHED: H. Moss. *Chinese Snuff Bottles*, No. 2, p. 28, fig. 5

This bottle clearly owes its inspiration to the group of Chinese Imperial Ivories discussed above. Nevertheless it is carved in a distinctively Japanese style, particularly visible in the stylised diaper. The method of construction, with a separately fitted neck, is another firm indication of Japanese origins.

217

217

Amber; of natural pebble form applied overall in *shibayama* style, using gilt lacquer, mother-of-pearl, turquoise and coral to depict dense clusters of flowering plants and bamboo springing from rockwork; *height: 5.8cm*.

Japan; 1850-1900

> PROVENANCE: Sotheby's London, 2nd December, 1985, lot 123

This technique of decoration is reputed to have been invented by the Shibayama Family in Japan during the early eighteenth century. The style reached a height of popularity in the second half of the nineteenth century and this bottle, originally a Chinese amber pebble bottle, was probably decorated during this latter period.

Bottles with this type of decoration are of outstanding rarity. Only one other similar has been recorded, formerly in the Bob Stevens and Eric Young Collections[1].

1. Bob C. Stevens. *The Collector's Book of Snuff Bottles*, no. 1025.

218

Ivory; carved with a continuous scene depicting numerous figures in a landscape, formed by trees, rocky ledges and clouds, the base signed *Kenkoku*, matching stopper; *height: 7.2cm*.

Japanese; 1860-1920

Ivory, although a valuable material in the Orient, never possessed the same innate elegance or symbolism as bamboo. Items of ivory therefore required a more dazzling level of artistry in order to capture the cultivated mind.

This bottle, with its minutely detailed figures and trees, the leaves pierced and undercut, succeeds perfectly in this task.

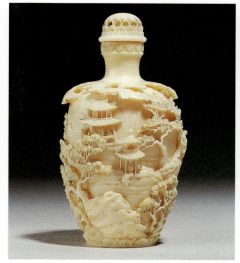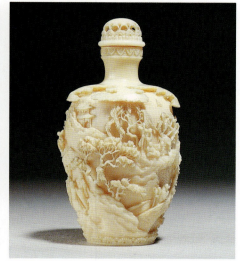

218

219

219

Boxwood; carved in deep relief with a continuous scene depicting a large number of figures seated in small groups on rocky promontories overlooking a fast-flowing stream, a tall pavilion to one side, *height: 6.2cm.*

Japan; 1850-1900

A small group of bottles exists, mainly carved in ivory or horn, which are very similar in style to this example. The ivory bottles, in particular, exhibit characteristic Japanese features in the treatment of the low relief carving on the shoulders[1], enabling the origin of the whole group to be pin-pointed.

1. Bob C. Stevens. *The Collector's Book of Snuff Bottles,* nos. 778 and 779.

Porcelain
and
Stoneware

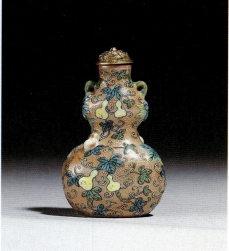

220

Porcelain; of small size and double-gourd form, decorated overall with a moulded fruiting gourd vine, reserved on an iron-red ground filled with a gilt classic scroll, the base inscribed within a square with the seal mark *Qianlong nianzhi* (*made in the Qianlong period*); *height: 4.9cm*.

Jingdezhen imperial ware; Qianlong period, 1736-1795

PROVENANCE: J.&J. Collection
                          Eric Young
                          Sotheby's London, 3rd March 1987, lot 64

It is very rare to find a porcelain snuff bottle with the correct mark of Qianlong. The Chinese, as a rule, did not lavish much care on porcelain snuff bottles because, as a medium, porcelain was so much better suited to bowls, vases and other larger vessels which could make full use of the plasticity and translucency of the medium.

Nevertheless, because of the very large number of well documented porcelain wares made at Jingdezhen for imperial use and marked accordingly with reign marks, there is a wealth of comparative material available for study[1].

This bottle compares very well with the above group of porcelains. The reign mark on the base is neatly drawn and the top left-hand part of the character *zhi* contains the five-pronged element that is found on the marks of the finest Qianlong porcelains. The gilt-scroll ground on the bottle is well controlled and possesses a coherent line, the leaves are painted very much in similar style to those found on the related porcelain wares and the tones of the enamels are the correct shade of translucent green.

An identical bottle is in the Percival David Foundation, London, no. 836, illustrated by Lady David in the *Catalogue* of Ch'ing Enamelled wares in the Foundation, and another is in the Collection of Mr. and Mrs. James Li.

1. See *Illustrated Catalogue of Ch'ing Porcelain in the National Palace Museum, Republic of China.*

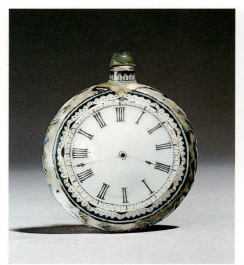

221

221

Porcelain; of flattened form moulded as a European pocket-watch, the face slightly raised, the shoulders with scattered scrolls; *height: 5.8cm.*

Qianlong period, 1736-1795

    PROVENANCE: H.G. Beasley (bought in Peking, 12th May, 1926)
                              Mac Beasley
                              Sotheby's London, 2nd July 1984, lot 5
                              Emily B. Curtis

Snuff Bottles of this form are extremely rare. The style of painting and the tones of the enamels are consistent with a Qianlong dating, and compare well with other wares of the period particularly those made for export.

222

Porcelain; A Pair of bottles each decorated in 'famille-rose' enamels; one with figures seated around a table, attendants on the reverse preparing food and drink; the other depicting a boy bringing a vase of flowers to a seated dignitary, flowering magnolia and peonies on the reverse, the decoration bordered by gilt-decorated underglaze-blue petals and *ruyi* heads, the base inscribed with the seal *Jiaqing nianzhi* (*made in the Jiaqing period*); *height: 6.9cm.*

Jingdezhen imperial ware; Jiaqing period, 1796-1820

    PROVENANCE: Hugh Moss
                              The Belfort Collection

    EXHIBITED: Hong Kong Museum of Art, October, 1978
                              Arcade Chaumet, Paris, June 1982, *Catalogue*, nos. 7&8

    PUBLISHED: Hong Kong Museum. *Catalogue*, no. 113.
                              V. Jutheau. *Tabatières Chinoises*, p. 82, fig. 2

The decoration on these bottles compares very closely with that found on other Jiaqing-marked imperial wares. The slightly shaded green enamel ground, the line technique used on the hands and faces and the tones of the enamels are all what one would expect for a genuine item of the period. The seal marks are neat with the bottom two strokes in the character, *zhi*, drawn separately, another sign of imperial quality.[1] Another pair from this set, from the Stempel Collection, was sold at Sotheby's New York, 11th October 1979, lot 63.

1. See the footnote to number 220 above.

222

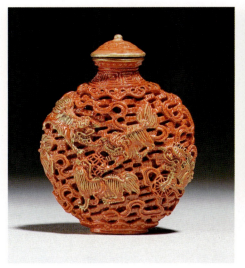
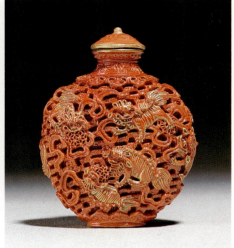

223

223

Porcelain; moulded overall with numerous Buddhist lions playing with brocade balls on a pierecd cloud scroll ground, covered in a coral-red glaze with the lions outlined in gilt, the base inscribed in gilt with the four character seal *Jiaqing nianzhi (made in the Jiaqing period)*; *height: 6.6cm*.

Jingdezhen; Jiaqing period, 1796-1820

A large group of porcelain snuff bottles exists which are moulded in the style of the imperial ivory bottles discussed above. It is likely that the earliest of this group were made from moulds directly taken from the ivory bottles. The ivory bottles date from the second half of the eighteenth century and moulding of the porcelain copies must have started soon after.

This particular bottle is crisply moulded indicating an early moulding. The moulds were used frequently and as the years passed the definition of the detail became less well defined. The seal marks found on this group do not have the neat quality of the preceding examples and this would tend to suggest a non-imperial destination. The glaze in this case is imitating coral, but other examples from the same mould would have been glazed to imitate other semi-precious substances such as ivory, lapis-lazuli and turquoise.

224

Porcelain; moulded on each side with nine dragons in differing attitudes emerging from the sea to grasp a flaming pearl, covered overall in a creamy white glaze; *height: 6cm*.

Jingdezhen; Jiaqing period, 1796-1820

PROVENANCE: Lilla S. Perry
Eric Young
Sotheby's London, 3rd March, 1987, lot 60

PUBLISHED: Lilla Perry. *Chinese Snuff Bottles*, p. 84, fig. 65

The crispness of the decoration on this bottle is outstanding. It is likely that it was enhanced by additional carving after being released from the mould.

224

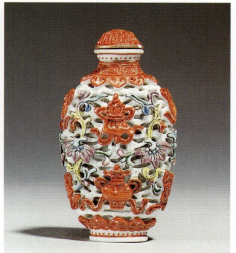

225

225

Porcelain; moulded overall with the eight Buddhist Emblems, enamelled in 'famille-rose' colours and reserved on a ground of white cloud scrolls, the base inscribed in iron-red with the seal mark *Jiaqing nianzhi* (*made in the Jiaqing period*); *height: 7.6cm*.

Jingdezhen; Jiaqing period, 1796-1820

The eight Buddhist Emblems consisted of the Wheel, the Conch, the Umbrella, the Lotus, the Vase, the Paired Fish, the Canopy and the Endless Knot.

226

226

Porcelain; moulded as the figure of Liu Hai, standing with a string of cash draped over one shoulder, the three-legged toad resting on one of his feet; *height: 7.2cm.*

Jingdezhen; Jiaqing period, 1796-1820

> PROVENANCE: Dr. Paula Hallett
> Sotheby's New York, 27th June, 1986, lot 2

A small group of figural snuff bottles is known of which Liu Hai is one of the most popular. The best of the group, of which this is one, date from the nineteenth century and the quality of the moulding declines over the following fifty years.

227

Porcelain; moulded on each side with erotic scenes, enamelled in 'famille-rose' colours on a gold ground; *height: 5.5cm.*

Jingdezhen; Jiaqing period, 1796-1820

> PROVENANCE: The Belfort Collection

> EXHIBITED: Arcade Chaumet, Paris, June 1982, *Catalogue*, no. 41

It is unusual to find an erotic-subject snuff bottle of such good quality as this one. The colours are vivid and the moulding has crispness and vitality.

227

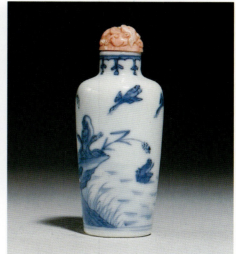

228

228

Porcelain; a Pair of bottles decorated in underglaze-blue with a gaggle of geese feeding beneath millet sprays, two further birds on the reverse swooping downwards, the base inscribed with the hall mark *siyi tang zhi (made in the hall of meditation and constancy)*; *height: 6.6cm*.

Jingdezhen; 1800-1850

PROVENANCE: Hugh Moss
              The Belfort Collection

EXHIBITED: Arcade Chaumet, Paris, June 1982, *Catalogue*, no. 1 and 2

PUBLISHED: V. Jutheau. *Tabatières Chinoises*, p. 89

The Chinese have followed the practice for centuries of giving names to their residence, to areas within them, or to private studios. These names were either propitious or had scholarly connotations which only the erudite would understand. Works of art were often marked with these names either to signify that they were used there or that they were made there, and these names are generally referred to as hall marks.

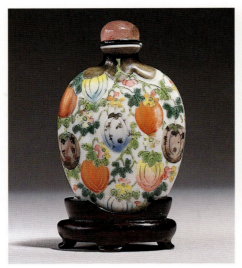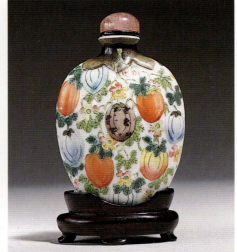

229

229

Porcelain; of flattened form moulded as a melon with low relief leaves on the shoulders and lightly fluted sides, enamelled overall with fruiting melon vines; *height: 6.7cm.*

Jingdezhen; Jiaqing period, 1796-1820

    PROVENANCE: The Belfort Collection

    PUBLISHED: V. Jutheau. *Tabatières Chinoises*, p. 85

The delicacy of the painting and the tones of the enamels on this bottle are entirely consistent with a Jiaqing dating.

230

Porcelain; of flattened disc shape enamelled on each side with fruiting melon scrolls on an iron-red ground; *height: 7cm.*

Jingdezhen; 1820-1880

    PROVENANCE: Gerd Lester

The enamelled colours on this bottle are slightly more strident than those on the preceding examples and the fruiting scroll lacks the fluidity demonstrated by number 229 above. These are both indications of a date of manufacture well into the nineteenth century.

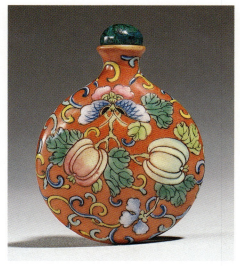

230

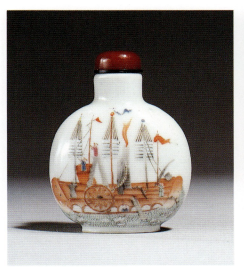

231

231

Porcelain; enamelled on front with a scene depicting Queen Victoria receiving a delegation, the reverse with a European three-masted sailing ship, the base with the four character seal mark *Daoguang nianzhi* (*made in the Daoguang period*); *height: 5.8cm*.

Jingdezhen; Daoguang period, 1821-1850

PROVENANCE: Gerd Lester

European subjects were rarely depicted during the Daoguang reign, but this subject may have been inspired by the close contact between the British and the Chinese during the 1840's.

232

232

Porcelain; enamelled in puce with a continuous scene depicting a carp jumping from the waves and a dragon in the clouds above, the base with the four character seal mark *Daoguang nianzhi* (*made in the Daoguang period*); *height: 5.5cm.*

Jingdezhen; Daoguang period, 1821-1850

    PROVENANCE: Gerd Lester

This type of enamel decoration is unusual on a snuff bottle. It was first developed during the Qianlong reign, possibly to heighten decoration in underglaze copper-red, where the red had mis-fired, but the technique soon became used in its own right. The rounded shape is typical for bottles of the period.

This bottle symbolises the dream of the scholar, before the civil service examinations, of passing and becoming a mandarin.

233

Porcelain; decorated in underglaze-blue and white on each side with a scaly dragon chasing a flaming pearl amongst clouds, the base with the four character seal mark *Daoguang nianzhi* (*made in the Daoguang period*); *height: 5.6cm.*

Jingdezhen; Daoguang period, 1821-1850

    PROVENANCE: Gerd Lester

A classic example of blue and white painting of the Daoguang period with its broad brushstrokes in a watery wash.

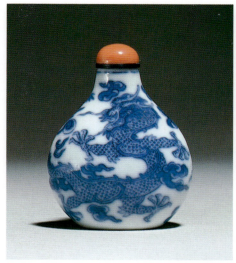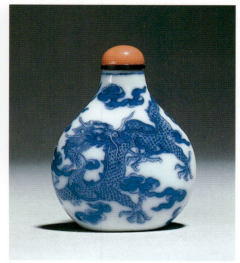

233

234

234

Porcelain; decorated in underglaze-blue and copper-red with severval fan-tailed carp swimming amongst aquatic fronds, the base similarly decorated; *height: 8.2cm.*

Jingdezhen; 1800-1850

The tone of the copper-red decoration in this case is exceptionally vivid and the painting is executed with unusual vigour and freedom. Enormous numbers of blue and white and copper-red decorated snuff bottles were made throughout the nineteenth century, some with real merit, and this is a group which deserves further study.

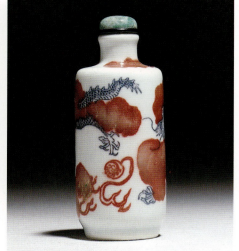

235

235

Porcelain; decorated with a dragon in underglaze-blue writhing in and out of vivid underglaze-red clouds; *height: 7.3cm.*

Jingdezhen; 1820-1850

The style of painting on this bottle relates very closely to that of number 234 above. Underglaze copper-red was extremely difficult to fire successfully, the results more often than not being a muddy greyish tone.

236

Porcelain; carved with a coiled dragon chasing a flaming pearl on a pierced ground of clouds, the inner core of the bottle visible within, the base incised *Wang Bingrong zhi (made by Wang Bingrong); height: 6.2cm.*

By Wang Bingrong, Jingdezhen; 1820-1860

A number of private kilns were in production at Jingdezhen during the nineteenth century, and many of the works of these kilns were signed by the craftsmen who made them. Amongst the best known of these were Wang Bingrong and Chen Guozhi, both of whom specialised in making small items for the scholar's table such as brushpots, seal paste boxes and snuff bottles.

These works were usually moulded, or potted in the case of larger vessels, and the designs were then embellished with carving whilst still in the unfired state. They were then fired once, leaving them in an unglazed state, in the biscuit. Their texture in this state is slightly rough to the touch and this was evidently pleasing to the Chinese as a large number of the works of these two Schools have been left unglazed in the biscuit.

Occasionally, as with this bottle, a thin coloured glaze has been applied, and a number of bottles of this design are known, in a variety of monochrome glazes. The works of both artists were often copied but the originals, as in this case, are defined by the sharpness of the carving and the vigour of the designs.

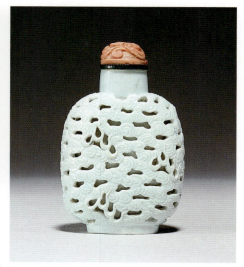

236

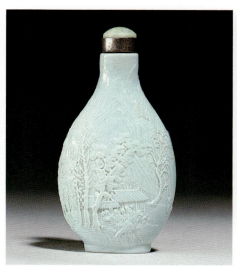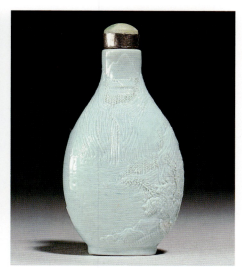

237

237

Porcelain; carved with a continuous scene depicting a pavilion nestling beneath pine and maple trees, the reverse with a tall waterfall dropping into a lake, the base incised *Chen Guozhi* (*made by Chen Guozhi*); *height: 7.5cm.*

By Chen Guozhi, Jingdezhen; 1820-1860

PROVENANCE: Mr. and Mrs. L. Kardos
Sotheby's New York, 1st July, 1985, lot 5

PUBLISHED: *Connaissance des Arts*, Paris, November, 1971, no. 237, pp. 102-109

The landscape on this bottle is a classic literati scene evoking as it does the tranquil sounds of a waterfall and the countryside.

175

238

238

Porcelain; carved on front with a crane, its wings displayed, perched on a jagged rock rising from the waves, the waves continuing on the reverse with the sun partly hidden by clouds above, covered overall in a pale lime-green glaze with the beak and legs of the bird picked out in black, the base signed *Chang Menshao zhi* (*made by Chang Menshao*); *height: 7.5cm.*

By Chang Menshao, Jingdezhen; 1820-1860

PROVENANCE: Christies London, 19th December, 1986

A lesser-known artist in the Wang Bingrong style, nevertheless this bottle exhibits a distinctively individual style with a certain angularity in the design which lends vigour to the whole concept.

239

Porcelain; carved on front with peony sprays and on the reverse with orchids, covered overall in a pale yellowish-green glaze, the base incised *Yucheng*; *height: 7.1cm.*

By Li Yucheng, Jingdezhen; 1820-1860

PROVENANCE: Albert Pyke
Mr. and Mrs. L. Kardos
Sotheby's New York, 1st July, 1985, lot 8

PUBLISHED: *Connaissance des Arts*, Paris, November, 1971, pp. 102-109

Li Yucheng is one of the rarest and most highly esteemed of the group of porcelain carvers who worked around the middle of the nineteenth century.

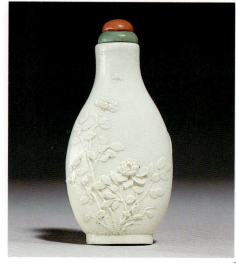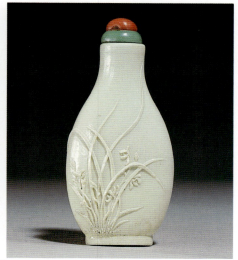

239

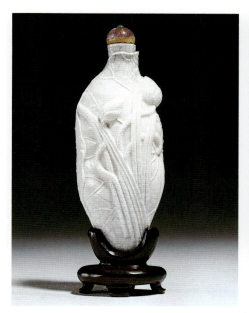

240

240

Porcelain; moulded in the form of a curled lotus leaf, the sides enveloped by the stalk and slender leaves, covered overall in a crackled greyish glaze; *height: 9cm.*

Jingdezhen; 1840-1880

This type of glaze is an imitation of the *ge* glazes which were highly valued on the stonewares of the Song Dynasty (A.D. 960-1279). Compare with the ivory bottle number 186 above.

241

241

Stoneware; enamelled on front with a spray of chrysanthemum and on the reverse with prunus, both on a blue enamel ground; *height: 5.7cm*.

Yixing ware; 1750-1820

> PROVENANCE: The Ko Collection
> Christies London, 12th July 1972

Yixing, in the province of Jiangsu in the Yangtze Valley, became a noted centre for the manufacture of pottery wares during the late Ming period. The proximity of rich local deposits of suitable clays and a prosperous community led to these wares becoming much prized and cultivated by members of the literati class. Yixing was most famous for its teapots, but all manner of small scholastic articles, often in rustic style were produced.

Many snuff bottles were produced in Yixing, but in general not before the nineteenth century. This particular bottle, however, with its boldly painted flowering sprays could well be earlier. The balanced use of space and the simplicity of the designs compare well with the style of the enamelled Yixing wares in the National Palace Museum, Taiwan, which date from the eighteenth century[1], and also with the style of 'famille-rose' painting then current in Jingdezhen.

1. *Illustrated Catalogue of Ch'ing Dynasty Porcelain in the National Palace Museum, Republic of China*, K'ang Hsi Wares and Yung Ch'eng Ware, pls 43/47.

242

Stoneware; of flattened form with fluted sides simulating a melon, enamelled on front with a bird perched on a branch of prunus and on the reverse with bamboo and chrysanthemum; *height: 6.7cm*.

Yixing ware; 1820-1880

> PROVENANCE: Gerd Lester

It is instructive to compare the decoration of this bottle with that of the preceding one. The design is much stiffer, the blossoms are less subtly outlined in white and areas of space have been loosely filled with scattered sprigs, whereas the decoration on the earlier bottle fills the space available naturally and with fluidity. Nevertheless, the unusual form and the overall effect of this bottle are pleasing.

242

243

243

Stoneware; modelled as an egg-plant with the stalk and leaves added in a darker slip, with a matching stopper; *length 8cm*.

Yixing ware; 1820-1880

Fruit or vegetable forms are rarely found in snuff bottles but are not uncommon amongst Yixing wares in general.

Various Metals

244

Bronze; with a concave circular panel on each side, enclosed by slender incised dragons confronted on a 'flaming pearl', the shoulders with small raised panels incised with a floral sprig, the base engraved *shunzhi bingxu cheng rongzheng zhi; height: 5.7cm.*

North China; 1646, Shunzhi period

PROVENANCE: Lilla S. Perry
Bob C. Stevens

EXHIBITED: Mikimoto Hall, Tokyo, October 1978, *Catalogue*, no. 341

PUBLISHED: Lilla S. Perry. *Chinese Snuff Bottles*, p. 27, no. 7
Bob. C. Stevens. The *Collector's Book of Snuff Bottles*, no. 808
Journal of the I.C.S.B.S., December 1978, p. 44, fig. 341

This bottle belongs to a small group of incised bronze bottles, of which approximately twenty have been recorded, made by Cheng Rongzhang between 1644 and 1654.

It has been asserted by Schuyler Cammann[1], and more recently by Emily Byrne Curtis[2], that this group of bottles is more likely to date from the nineteenth century than from the mid-seventeenth century, as inscribed. Nevertheless, a careful examination of the arguments put forward by these two authors and a comparison with the decorative motifs on other wares of the seventeenth and nineteenth centuries should leave one in no doubt as to their authenticity as dated.

Cammann states, quite correctly, that one of the greatest aids to dating an object, in the absence of documentary evidence, is to compare the decorative motifs on that object with similar motifs on objects whose date is beyond doubt. He uses the dragons found on the majority of this group of bronze bottles as a starting point, and concludes that these dragons are typical of the way the Chinese depicted dragons in the nineteenth century.

A study of the dragons, clouds and sprigs depicted on these bottles in fact reveals quite clearly their close similarity to similar motifs found on seventeenth century ceramics and bronzes. The dragons are slender and freely drawn, with great vigour whereas nineteenth century dragons are invariably fat and stiff, with short tails. The scales of the dragons are ring-punched, a seventeenth century technique used by bronze makers, including the Hu Wenming School, whereas the scales of dragons found on nineteenth century dragons on dated bronze censers tend to be cross-hatched and not ring-punched.

The cloud scrolls and floral sprigs on the bottles, similarly compare much more closely with the examples on seventeenth century ceramics than with those to be found on the later wares.

Curtis questions both the structure and the patination of these bottles. With regard to the structure she asks how the earliest of all snuff bottles could spring into existance in a fully developed form with an integral saucer panel. However, this form, with an integral saucer, becomes much less common on later bottles, probably because the use of a separate snuff dish became preferred.

With regard to the patination, Curtis illustrates an example originally in the Martin Schoen Collection, which was illustrated in 1952 having been recently cleaned and again in 1976 by which time it had acquired the 'accepted' patina. Whilst this bottle had undoubtedly darkened over the period in question its patination remained substantially different from that of the uncleaned bottles. The uncleaned examples exhibit a degree of natural wear and tear and decomposition in the surface of the metal commensurate with a seventeenth century date, and once again, a comparison with the patination on other bronzes of this period and the nineteenth century is instructive.

Finally, one should examine the motives for creating any group of fakes. Curtis finds it plausable that an individual who wished to create a market for his wares would choose the earliest possible date for a snuff bottle as this would appeal to a collector of rareties.

However, in the nineteenth century there was no collectors' market for snuff bottles, that would have been likely to have shown interest in a group of crudely made metal wares in a cheap material that copied no known originals (which we must accept if the whole group was fake). In addition, a close study of the Chengrong Zhang group demonstrates a coherent artistic development between 1644 and 1654 which is entirely consistent with a genuine group but would demonstrate a degree of sophistication in a fake far beyond the requirements of an object which would at that time have had little value.

The question of the actual area of China in which these bottles were manufactured is more difficult. Curtis points out that there is no documentary evidence that the Manchu, in North China, took snuff. However this is not the case[3].

The Manchu descended from the north and toppled the Ming Dynasty in 1644 to form the Qing Dynasty, of which the emperor, Shunzhi, was the first ruler. Nevertheless, the circumstantial evidence in favour of the North being the likely area of manufacture is very strong. The use of tobacco was widespread enough in the North to provoke an edict banning its use for smoking in 1639[4], and a knowledge of smoking implies a knowledge of snuff. The North was the seat of government and although there is evidence that snuff was also disseminated in the South, particularly by the Jesuits, the great bulk of Jesuit interest was aimed directly at the seat of government and it is not unreasonable to assume that snuff, at that time a sought after commodity in Europe, would have figured prominently in gifts to the court. It therefore seems likely that these bottles would have been made to meet the demand in the North, and certainly the pattern of extent wares overwhelmingly supports this view.

1. Schuyler V.R. Cammann. *Miniature Art from Old China: Chinese Snuff Bottles from the Montclair Art Museums* (Montclair, New Jersey) 60, no. 35.
2. E. B. Curtis. 'The Impact of the West — Part III,' *Journal* of the I.C.S.B.S., Spring 1987, p. 4 *et seq.*
3. Shen Yu in his Chiuyin tsa-chi, (miscellaneous Notes of the Autumn Shade Studio), 1837, remarks 'Snuff was introduced at the beginning of this (Qing) Dynasty and initially was popular among the Manchus and court officials'.
4. For a detailed review of the Chinese sources relating to Snuff-taking see G. Tsang, 'Chinese views on Snuff' in the *Catalogue of Chinese Snuff Bottles*, Hong Kong Museum of Art, August 1977, where he lists numerous early Qing references to Snuff-taking.

245

Bronze; covered in gilding and cast on each side with the eight Daoist emblems, the fan, the sword, the double-gourd, the castanets, the flower-basket, the bamboo tube, the drum, and the flute, all on a ring-punched ground; *height: 7.2cm.*

Qianlong period, 1736-1795

PROVENANCE: The Belfort Collection

EXHIBITED: Arcade Chaumet, Paris, June 1982, *Catalogue*, no. 256

PUBLISHED: V. Jutheau. *Tabatières Chinoises*, p. 51, fig. 2

The quality and style of casting of this bottle compare very closely with that found on numerous *Qianlong*-marked bronze wares, and particularly with the gilt-bronze details often found on cloisonné enamel wares of the period. The ring-punched ground is also typical of early qing bronze work. It is rare to find a snuff bottle of this material.

The emblems depicted on this bottle belong respectively to each of the Eight Immortals.

246

Copper; inlaid on each side in silver wire with an inscription in a differing style of calligraphy, the body hinged at the foot to allow it to open into two halves; *height: 5.8cm.*

Daoguang period, dated 1834

PROVENANCE: Albert Pyke
Mr. and Mrs. L. Kardos,
Sotheby's New York, 1st July, 1985, lot 15

EXHIBITED: Vancouver Museum, 1977

PUBLISHED: *Connaissance des Arts*, Paris, November, 1971, pp. 102-109

As this bottle opens into two halves it would not have been a satisfactory container for snuff. It was probably used as a container for secret messages or as an examination crib.

The inscription on the front reads: 'your eyes can be twice as clear; four directions (the whole universe) are opening up; this gentleman (a reference to the bottle) provides me with genuine enjoyment. Its reputation and value equals that of an entire city. Kefu gave this bottle to Douhou in the Chrysanthemum month, 1834.'

The inscription on the reverse reads: 'This mirror shows us love for the features of beautiful women.'

247

Silver and silver-gilt; cast on each side with a central gilt dragon medallion set on a reticulated ground of stylised scrolls, the shoulders with a narrow classic scroll band repeated on the foot and neck; *height: 6.2cm.*

1860-1910

This bottle, with its use of pierced metal and the stopper inset with turquoise beads, displays considerable Mongolian or Tibetan influence in its styling.

245

246

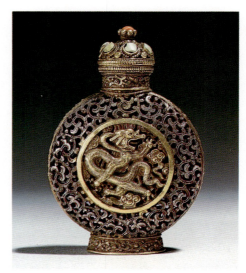

247

Inside-Painted
Rock Crystal
and
Glass

248

Rock crystal; painted on the inside with a figure in a sampan, tall mountains in the distance, the shoulders with rockwork and grass, the reverse with an inscription; *height: 5.3cm.*

Attributed to Gan Xuanwen; circa 1815-1830

    PROVENANCE: Heflene Collection

The first recorded mention of painting inside a snuff bottle occurs in a Paris auction catalogue from 1810[1] and the earliest recorded such snuff bottle still in existance is dated to the Jiaqing reign, 1816[2].

Whilst there is no means of identifying the artist of the Paris bottle, this latter bottle is by Gan Xuanwen, signed, and painted in a a very distinctive style. The bottle itself is of small size, in rock crystal, rectangular in form and painted with a grisaille landscape on one side and an inscription on the reverse.

A fairly large group of similar bottles exists and although some are signed by Gan Xuanwen, some are signed in other names and some remain unsigned, the similarities in style and execution throughout are such that it is likely that the majority are by the same hand.

A.O. Blishen traces the development of Gan Xuanwen in an illustrated article in the *Journal* of the International Chinese Snuff Bottle Society[3]. The latest date he records for a work which is clearly by this artist is 1864, although he does illustrate two later bottles, from 1869 and 1871 which are possibly by another hand, or possibly by Gan in old age.

Gan Xuanwen is on record as an artist of the Lingnan School, which was based in Guangzhou and a handscroll by him, dating to the Jiaqing reign (1796-1820) is in the possession of The Chinese University of Hong Kong.

The bottle illustrated here has many close similarities in the manner of painting the mountains and in the calligraphy on the reverse to the early signed examples by Gan Xuanwen, allowing a confident attribution to him in this case.

1. Victor Graham. 'Chinese Snuff Bottles: The French Connection'. *Journal* of the I.C.S.B.S, December 1979, p. 9.
2. Hong Kong Museum, *Catalogue*, no. 216, October 1978.
3. A.O. Blishen. 'Early Inside-painted Snuff Bottles by Kan Huan-wen'. *Journal* of the I.C.S.B.S., December 1974, p. 12.

249

Rock crystal; painted on the inside with a sage and attendant walking through a mountain landscape, a rustic bridge in the foreground, the shoulders with bamboo and rocks, the reverse with a lengthy inscription; *height: 5.3cm*.

Attributed to Gan Xuanwen; circa 1820-1830

The composition of the landscape, the economical use of the brush to suggest the distant mountains and the confident treatment of the rockwork cliffs on this bottle all point to a fine artist, well trained in the techniques and goals of Chinese painting.

A bottle in very similar line drawing style with meticulous minute detailing, signed Gan Xuanwen, was exhibited at the Hong Kong Museum of Art, October 1978, *Catalogue*, no. 217.

250

Rock crystal; painted on the inside with a hatted figure in a mountain landscape, the reverse with an inscription, signed *Gu Kaijiao*; *height: 5.2cm*.

Attributed to Gan Xuanwen; circa 1830-1860

PROVENANCE: Hugh Moss
Eric Young
Sotheby's London, 3rd March 1987, lot 137

PUBLISHED: A.O. Blishen. *Journal* of the I.C.S.B.S., December 1974, p. 16, figs. 15/16

The brushwork on this bottle is more fluid than that of the preceding example and this, together with the touches of red colour and the bold calligraphy on the reverse, points towards a slightly later date of execution.

The name Gu Kaijiao on the bottle is probably that of the poet whose poem is inscribed, but the similarities in style of brushwork and calligraphy are so close to that on two signed bottles by Gan Xuanwen illustrated by Moss in *Snuff Bottles of China*, nos. 370 and 371, that an attribution to the same artist for this bottle is possible.

249

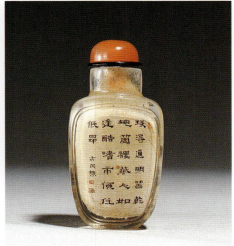

250

251

Rock crystal; painted on the inside with a scene of scholars gathered in a clearing with tall cliffs and a waterfall in the distance, beneath the inscription *xiuxie tu (Painting of a Purification Party), fang song ren ben, (imitating the version of a Song Dynasty person), Erzhong wrote this*, with a seal, *Ding*, the reverse with the complete text of Wang Xizhi's Lanting Preface, signed, *Erzhong made this at Jingmen, tenth month of 1884*, with seal *Erzhong*; height: 6.7cm.

By Ding Erzhong; 1884-1904

    PROVENANCE: The Ko Collection

Ding Erzhong is regarded as the most accomplished of all the artists who practised the art of painting inside snuff bottles.

He is recorded in a Chinese source as a native of Hebei and a noted seal carver, and his other name was Shangyu[1]. He was a member of the scholar class, a trained artist and from the very small number of his works which are recorded, (fewer than fifty), and the dedications found on many of these, it seems clear that he did not paint commercially but only for friends or family.

This was very much in the tradition of Chinese painting; it was regarded as an anathema to charge for any work as this would reduce the art to the status of a mere craft.

The dating of this bottle, 1884, presents a puzzle, as all the other recorded works by Ding date from between 1895 and 1905. However the quality of painting on this example is as fine as on any of the later works both in its composition and in the skill with which the brush-strokes are controlled. This is clearly not an early or exploratory work but is indeed one of Ding's masterpieces.

There would appear to be three possible explanations; first, the dating is correct (and there is no record elsewhere of Ding having used incorrect dates), in which case we shall have to revise radically the parameters of our dating of this artist; or, second, he painted the bottle at a later date, possibly around 1900, and dated his copy of the inscription to commemorate an important landmark earlier in his career; or third, he made a mistake with the cyclical characters, (not uncommon amongst the literati) in which case he could have meant either 1894 or 1904.

One other bottle by Ding, also painted on the rarely used rock crystal with the complete Lanting Preface, is recorded in the Collection of Mrs. Carl Kreuger, dated 1902[2]. It is interesting to note that both on the Kreuger example and on this bottle, Ding has inscribed the characters *xiuxie tu* in a similarly eccentric fashion. This factor, together with the maturity of the earlier example, which compares closely to number 260 below, and the complete lack of any other examples of Ding's work recorded between 1884 and 1895 tend to point towards the dating of 1884 being either a commemorative date or an error, rather than an actual dating, with the date of execution being around 1900-1904.

252

A final resolution of this problem awaits the discovery of further examples of Ding's works, but there is no doubt of the importance of this bottle in the study of Ding's *œuvre* as a whole.

The importance of the Lanting Preface and Wang Xizhi as the pinnacle of Chinese calligraphy is discussed above (number 179) and an example of the preface copied by Ma Shaoxuan is illustrated at number 288.

1. See G. Tsang & H. Moss. 'Snuff Bottles of the Ch'ing Dynasty'. Hong Kong Museum of Art. October 1978, *Catalogue*, p. 37.
2. Bob C. Stevens. *The Collector's Book of Snuff Bottles*, no. 882.

252

Glass; painted on the inside with a monkey crouched beneath the trunk of a tree, the shoulders with an inscription, *may your family bring forth princes and noblemen for a hundred generations, spring of the year bingshen, made for the elder brother Xuanfu*, the signature and the seal, Erzhong; the reverse with a mounted huntsman in pursuit of a deer; *height: 6.1cm*.

By Ding Erzhong; Spring 1896

This bottle depicts unusual subject matter for this artist, who tended to prefer the traditionally accepted landscape and still-life scenes. The colours of the palette are also unusual being predominantly bluish in tone rather than the series of pale olive-greens, russets and grisaille which Ding most often favoured.

253

253

Glass; painted on the inside on front with a still-life scene of a bronze vessel with a spray of blossom planted within, an ornamental rock to one side, the shoulders with an inscription *fu gui shou gao (riches and longevity), painted by Erzhong in Xuannan*, the artist's seal, *Ding*, and the date, the reverse with two figures in a pavilion in a mountain landscape, the signature, *Erzhong*, and the seal *Ding*; *height: 6cm.*

By Ding Erzhong; Spring, 1896

    PROVENANCE: Gerd Lester

A study of the series of bottles by Ding Erzhong in this exhibition will reveal an improvement in the confidence and control of his brush-strokes as the years proceed.

One of the most important criteria in judging Chinese painting is the line and confidence exhibited by the artist in his brush-strokes, and in this area Ding excelled. This comparatively early bottle already shows fine brush-work, particularly in the execution of the ornamental rock and the sweep of the hills, but it is still some way from the superb control of the bottle, number 263 below, from 1904.

254

Glass; painted on the inside with a group of figures walking beside a lake with tall mountains in the distance, the signature and seal, *Erzhong* to one side, beneath the date written in a line, the reverse with two cranes on a mossy bank beneath a pine tree, the sun setting into the clouds above; *height: 5.8cm.*

By Ding Erzhong; 9th month, 1896

254

255

255

Glass; painted on the inside with Shou Lao reclining beside a recumbent stag, beneath a lengthy inscription signed *Erzhong* with seals and the date, the reverse with two cranes on a mossy bank beside two pine trunks and a short inscription *may you grow as old as the pine trees and cranes* signed *Ding Erzhong* with the date; *height: 6.4cm.*

By Ding Erzhong; Spring month, 1897

    PROVENANCE: Sotheby's London, 5th December 1983, lot 188

A rare figural subject for Ding. In this case the figure is finely drawn with the whole shape of his crouching body suggested by a few strokes, the touch of a master artist.

The inscription on the side with Shou Lao reads: *Painting of happiness, high rank and long life. I have at home a painting to decorate the hall, by Yuhu, and I have here copied its style on a small scale. Painted by Erzhong in Xuannan.*

256

256

Glass; painted on the inside with Shou Lao reclining against the back of a deer, beneath an inscription, the date and the signature *Ding Erzhong*, the reverse with two figures in a lakeside pavilion contemplating tall mountains, signed *Erzhong*, with an inscription *Trinket for the dear respected elder brother Youan*, and seal; *height: 6.2cm.*

By Ding Erzhong; 4th Month 1897

PROVENANCE: Sotheby's New York, 3rd November 1982, lot 275
Eric Young
Sotheby's London, 3rd March 1987, lot 148

The inscription on the side with Shou Lao reads: *as if by chance copying the outline drawing painting style of the Yuan painters, under the Southern window Shiqilou Meilanshanfang (a studio name).*
The use of the term 'elder brother', by an artist implies a dedication to a respected colleague rather than, literally, a member of the family.

257

Glass; painted on the inside with a continuous landscape scene, two figures on a bridge in the foreground, an inscription on the shoulders *for the approval of dear elder brother Shaobo*, together with the date and the signature *Erzhong; height: 6.7cm.*

By Ding Erzhong; Winter 1897

PROVENANCE: Hugh Moss

The brush-work on this bottle is very accomplished, particularly in the treatment of the foliage on the trees and the structure of the distant hills. In good Chinese painting it was regarded as essential not to repeat the shape or line of any rock formations. The trees are highlighted with orange, one of Ding's favourite mannerisms.

257

258

258

Glass; painted on the inside in grisaille with a continuous landscape scene, a group in the foreground riding in a boat, an inscription on the shoulders, *fang yuan ren fa yu tie yan zhai (imitating the style of a Yuan Dynasty person at the Iron Inkstone Studio)*, and the signature *Erzhong; height: 5.9cm*.

By Ding Erzhong; undated, circa 1897-1900

PROVENANCE: Dr. and Mrs. Louis Wolferz
Hugh Moss

In imitating a Yuan painting Ding reveals his own scholarly background. Although undated, this bottle fits stylistically into the middle period of Ding's recorded career as an artist in this genre. The treatment of the foilage is very similar to that of the preceding bottle.

259

259

Glass; painted on the inside with a crane in flight above the setting sun, flanked by an inscription, *A painting of the top official's rank, in imitation of the Yuan painters*, the signature *Erzhong* and the date, the reverse with a hart and a hind beneath a gnarled tree branch and the inscription, *in imitation of Xinluo Shanren's style*; height: 5.7cm.

By Ding Erzhong; 2nd Spring month 1899

    PROVENANCE: Arthur Gadsby
                        The Belfort Collection

    EXHIBITED: Arcade Chaumet, Paris, June 1982, *Catalogue*, no. 129

The composition of the painting of the two deer is perfectly balanced in the spacial relationship between the tree, the animals and the rock.

As with most of his bottles, Ding has signed his work on each side, a trait very rarely followed by other artists in this medium, but a natural action for a trained artist. In this series of bottles imitating the style of various well known painters, Ding once again reveals his own scholarly background.

260

Glass; painted on the inside with a river landscape scene beneath an inscription *for the perusal of Xiao-fang, the eminent Surveillance Commissioner*, signed *Erzhong* with seals, the reverse with two cranes on an ornamental rock beneath a gnarled pine trunk, the signature *Erzhong* and the date; *Height: 6cm.*

By Ding Erzhong; Winter 1899

The landscape on the front of this bottle compares closely with that on the rock crystal bottle with the Lanting Preface, number 251 above.

Ding's increasing confidence is well demonstrated by a comparison of his treatment of the two cranes and the pine tree on the reverse of this bottle with that of the same subject on numbers 254 and 255 above.

260

261

261

Glass; painted on the inside with a continuous scene depicting a deer, a crane and two song birds, framed by a mossy bank, flowers and a tree, an inscription on the shoulders, *For the respected dear elder brother Shaobo, in imitation of Xuanhe's paintings*, the signature and seals *Erzhong*, together with the date; *height: 5.8cm.*

By Ding Erzhong; Summer 1899

PROVENANCE: Gerd Lester

262

Rock crystal; painted on the inside with two ducks swimming beneath an overhanging branch of willow, an inscription, *intended to belong to the dear elder brother Yinnan*, the date and the signature, together with seals *Erzhong*, on the shoulders, a river landscape on the reverse; *height: 4.8cm*.

By Ding Erzhong; Autumn 1900

    PROVENANCE: Sotheby's New York, 3rd November 1982, lot 276
                          Eric Young
                          Sotheby's London, 3rd March 1987, lot 147

The two ducks is a hitherto unrecorded subject for Ding, and it is of interest to compare his version with that of Zhou Leyuan, number 267 below.

263

Glass; painted on the inside with a continuous river landscape scene, the sun setting behing distant mountains and small figures in the foreground, the shoulders inscribed *jiu ru tu (Painting of the Nine Likenesses)*, followed by the date and a further inscription, *imitating the technique of Hua Yisan for the worthy examination of Fangbo of Kongan, Ding Shangyu wrote this*; *height: 6.3cm*.

By Ding Erzhong; Winter 1904

    PUBLISHED: *Ceramics*, May/June 1986, Vol. 3, p. 140, fig. 4

Ding Shangyu was Ding Erzhong's other name, (see number 251 above), and the Nine Likenesses is an allusion to the poem *tian bao* in the chapter entitled *xiao ya* of the Zhou Dynasty classic of poetry. This poem because of the way in which it describes the countryside has come to signify a beautiful landscape.

This bottle is one of Ding's masterpieces. The varying form and line of the hills, the use of unpainted space to suggest water and the treatment of the distant misty mountains are all indicative of Chinese painting of the highest quality. This, together with the fluently written inscription and the allusion to a famous poem embodies 'The Three Perfections' most admired by the literati; painting, poetry and calligraphy.

262

263

Rock crystal; painted on the inside with a tree in a flowerpot flanked by a bronze vessel and an ornamental rock, beneath an inscription *Zhou Leyuan imitating the ancient style*, together with the date, the reverse with two figures seated beneath towering mountains, the shoulders inscribed, *for the enjoyment of fourth brother Songquan*; height: 7.2cm.

By Zhou Leyuan; 11th month, 1884

PROVENANCE: Gerd Lester

Zhou Leyuan is known to have painted inside snuff bottles between 1882 and 1893[1]. He is regarded as the founder of the Beijing School of artists in this genre which flourished between 1882 and the end of the Qing Dynasty in 1912. He was based in Beijing and is believed to have painted lanterns before he turned to snuff bottles.

This bottle dates from early in Zhou's career. Nevertheless it demonstrates much of the ability which was to make Zhou one of the greatest artists to paint inside bottles. The composition is well balanced and the brushwork is bold. The calligraphy is flowing, elegant and confident, always a hallmark of Zhou's, and it is clear that he must have had some formal training as an artist.

Although the inscription on this bottle is dedicated to 'fourth brother', this does not necessarily mean one of Zhou's family, and is more likely to have been a dedication to a member of another family.

1. H. Moss. *Chinese Snuff Bottles*, No. 4, p. 53.

Glass; painted on the inside with an ornamental rock flanked by jardinières, beneath an inscription, *for the amusement of seventh brother Yuedong*, the reverse signed *Zhou Leyuan* with the seal *yuan* and a figure in a sampan beneath a battlemented bridge partly hidden in the mist; height: 6.2cm.

By Zhou Leyuan; undated, circa 1889-1890

PROVENANCE: Emily Byrne Curtis

This bottle compares very closely in the style of the rockwork painting to that of a bottle dated 1889 and illustrated by Moss[1].

Zhou has been particularly successful on the reverse side in depicting the mist by leaving large areas of the surface unpainted, a technique much admired by connoisseurs of Chinese art and extremely difficult to achieve.

1. H. Moss. *Chinese Snuff Bottles*, No. 4, p. 61, fig. 18.

264

265

266

266

Rock crystal; painted on the inside with a crane on a mossy bank beside a fallen tree trunk, the reverse with a boy on a water-buffalo flying a kite, signed *Zhou Leyuan*, with seal *Leyuan* and a lengthy inscription; *height: 6cm.*

By Zhou Leyuan; undated, circa 1890

PROVENANCE: Hugh Moss
              Gerd Lester

EXHIBITED: Hong Kong Museum of Art, October 1978

PUBLISHED: H. Moss. *Chinese Snuff Bottles*, No. 4, p. 63, figs. 22/23
              Hong Kong Museum. *Catalogue*, no. 223

The reverse painting on this bottle is very similar to one dated 1890, illustrated by Moss[1]. The brush-work on the tail-feathers of the bird is executed with style and confidence and the characteristically sober-toned palette has witnessed the introduction of a pale blue in the bamboo which Zhou was to favour over the following two years.

1. H. Moss. *Chinese Snuff Bottles*, No. 4, p. 63, fig. 24.

267

Rock crystal; painted on the inside with two ducks paddling together beneath a leafy branch and the inscription, *written at Qimen in the eleventh month of 1891, Zhou Leyuan*, seal *yuanyin*, the reverse with a boy riding a water-buffalo, pavilions in the distance; *height: 6.3cm.*

By Zhou Leyuan; 11th month, 1891

A previously unrecorded subject for Zhou, in this case there is an unusually large area of unpainted space subtly highlighted by a faint touch of blue around the wading animal and the birds. The delicate pointing of the foliage on the side with the ducks is typical of Zhou's style and was never successfully copied by his imitators (see number 271).

267

268

268

Glass; painted on the inside with a mountain landscape scene beneath the inscription, *for the enjoyment of second brother Zhong Qian, Autumn 1891, painted at the Studio of Thirty-six documents*, the reverse with fishes beneath a mossy bank; *height: 6.8cm*.

By Zhou Leyuan; Autumn, 1891

The landscape on this bottle, inspired by an original of the famous 17th Century painter, Wang Shigu, is a variation of a subject which appears often in Zhou's work from 1891 and 1892.

It is likely that by this time Zhou was well established in his role and that this type of subject, with its scholarly connotations, would have had wide appeal.

The studio of the Fragrant Lotus-root was another studio recorded at which Zhou painted.

269

Rock crystal; painted on the inside with a continuous landscape scene, one side with a pine tree framing a waterfall and the sun setting beneath distant plains, the shoulders inscribed *for the enjoyment of Magistrate Zichun, written at Qimen, the eleventh month of 1891*, seal *Yuan*, the reverse with a differing pine tree framed by *lingzhi* fungus, a tall waterfall in the distance; *height: 6.5cm*.

By Zhou Leyuan; 11th month 1891

PROVENANCE: Hugh Moss

This bottle is one of Zhou's masterpieces. He has taken the popular pine in a landscape scene and completely transformed it. The pine tree on each side has been substantially increased in size to become the focus and the spreading branches extend the eye to embrace the differing facets of the landscape portrayed.

This is an example of a true artist at work. Rather than resting content with repetition he is exploring new ways of depicting a familiar scene. He has not allowed the confines of the space available to limit his vision and the broad and confident brush-strokes provide an insight into his spirit and character, a true test of the quality of the brush-stroke in Chinese eyes.

These attributes, also exhibited in many instances by Ding Erzhong, and to an extent by another artist in this medium, Zi Yici, place this group of artists apart from the remainder of the members of the Beijing School, the majority of whom, despite occasional masterpieces, were more in the nature of competent craftsmen producing paintings to satisfy popular demand.

270

Glass; painted on the inside with a continuous landscape scene, *after the style of Wang Shigu*, unsigned; *height: 6.1cm*.

Attributed to Zhou Leyuan; circa 1891-1893

PROVENANCE: Heflene Collection

Although unsigned, there is no doubt that this bottle is by Zhou Leyuan. The brush-work exhibited in the treatment of the pine needles and the hills is typical of his later work and the palette compares closely in tones with that of his last known bottle, dated to Spring, 1893[1].

No works by Zhou are recorded after this latter date and as the later paintings are of equal quality to the earlier ones, with no signs of a failing eye or lack of interest it is possible that Zhou died in this year.

1. H. Moss. *China Snuff Bottles*, N. 4, p. 71, fig. 39.

269

270

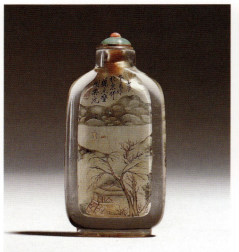
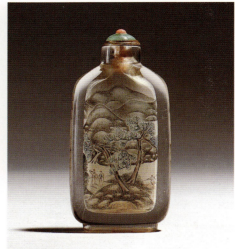

271

Rock crystal; painted on the inside with a continuous landscape scene, one side with a lakeside pavilion in the foreground beneath the inscription *made by Zhou Leyuan, Winter 1892, seal Leyuan*, the reverse with two figures beneath a cluster of pine trees; *height: 6.2cm*.

By the Ye Family, The Apricot Grove Studio; circa 1920-1930

PROVENANCE: Sotheby's London, 6th May 1986, lot 363

The enormous success enjoyed by Zhou Leyuan inspired numerous copies of his works. The majority of artists working in the medium produced bottles signed with Zhou's name, but none were so skilled as the members of the Ye Family, who worked at the Apricot Grove Studio.

The rise of this Studio is dealt with in more detail below, (number 274). However, a copy of a Zhou Leyuan work by Ye Zhongsan the Elder exists, dated as early as 1895[1].

The bottle illustrated here is a classic example of one of the Ye copies. At first glance it appears almost indistinguishable from an original work by Zhou. Nevertheless a comparison with the Zhou bottles illustrated above reveals differences.

The Ye treatment of the landscape hills is far less refined than that of Zhou. The outline is harsh, rather than formed from a natural brush-stroke merging with the sky and the mounds forming the body of the hills are stark rather than naturally and subtly shaded.

The foliage and pine needles of Zhou are likewise formed from fluent brush-strokes whereas the Ye use a meticulous line drawing technique also found on the detailing of the mossy bank.

The palette of the Ye tends towards either the slate-like colour of this example or a very characteristic bright pale green (see number 275), whereas Zhou's colours are a subtle mix of browns, greys and pale olive-green tones.

Finally, Zhou's calligraphy is confident and flowing as opposed to the rather awkward and untidy attempts of the Ye Family[2].

With regard to the dating of this particular bottle it is worth comparing it with the two landscape scenes by Ye Zhongsan the Elder illustrated below, (numbers 274 and 277). These, whilst exhibiting many of the typical Ye characteristics outlined nevertheless possess better calligraphy than that of the bottle illustrated. The sons of Ye, whilst succeeding in emulating the father's style very closely, used thinner and less flowing brush-strokes as is apparent from many bottles from the Apricot Grove Studio dating from the 1920s, when the sons were doing most of the painting. It is likely, therefore, that this bottle was executed during this later period.

1. H. Moss. 'The Apricot Grove Studio', *Journal* of the I.C.S.B.S., Autumn 1982, p. 16, fig. 20.
2. H. Moss. 'The Apricot Grove Studio', *Journal* of the I.C.S.B.S., Autumn 1984, p. 89, fig. 257.

272

Glass; painted on the inside with a continuous scene depicting numerous children at play in a schoolroom, the master seated at a table, beneath an inscription, *for the approval of respected elder brother Qinlu, the excellency, to correct*, signed *Ye Zhongsan, mid-winter, 1896, seal huayin*; *height: 5.9cm*.

By Ye Zhongsan the Elder; Mid-Winter, 1896

With Zhou Leyuan no longer working a vacuum was left which was filled by many artists. The best placed of these was Ye Zhongsan, who was probably a student of Zhou's.

The early works of Ye, from 1893 to 1895, were all copies of well known Zhou subjects, [1] but from 1896 onwards Ye began to develop his own style and repertoire.

This bottle is typical of Ye's early style, with its predominantly pale blue palette, which was used until around 1900, and the figures freely painted in almost caricature form, as opposed to the much stiffer figures of the later works (see number 279).

1. H. Moss. 'The Apricot Grove Studio', *Journal* of the I.C.S.B.S., p. 11/12, figs. 6-9.

273

273

Rock crystal; painted on the inside with a boy on a water-buffalo, beneath the signature, the date and the seal, *huayin*, the reverse with boys at play in a garden; *height: 5.9cm*.

By Ye Zhongsan the Elder; Autumn, 1896

Another bottle in classic early Ye style. The unusual shape of the bottle indicates that it was probably an undecorated rock crystal snuff bottle, dating from the early part of the century, which was brought by a client for decoration.

The use of the *huayin* seal by Ye was favoured during the early part of his career, with the less complicated *yin* seal becoming more common after about 1905.

274

Rock crystal; painted on the inside with a continuous scene depicting pine trees and pavilions in a mountain landscape, the shoulders with the signature, the date and the seal, *yin* ; *height: 6cm*.

By Ye Zhongsan the Elder; Summer, 1903

    PROVENANCE: Sotheby's London, 6th May 1986, lot 362

This landscape scene, developed from those of Zhou Leyuan, first appears in a bottle by Ye Dated 1897[1] and remained one of the most popular of the Ye catalogue.

Ye had three sons, Ye Bengzen, Ye Xiaofeng and Ye Bengqi, who each followed him into the profession of inside-painting[2]. The eldest son, Bengzen, was born in 1896 and began painting inside bottles in approximately 1912. The second son, Xiaofeng, was born in 1900 and began painting around 1920 and the third son, Bengqi, was born in 1908 and began his career around 1928.

The sons painted in the same style as the father, Ye Zhongsan the Elder, and with one exception, dated 1927, they signed their works in the father's name, before 1945. The elder Ye himself continued to paint until the early 1940's and it is therefore difficult, after about 1920 to distinguish the work of the individual hands.

Nevertheless, as the eldest son did not begin painting until 1912, any bottles with an earlier dating can safely be ascribed to the elder Ye himself. The family as a group painted at the Apricot Grove Studio in Beijing.

1. H. Moss. 'The Apricot Grove Studio', *Journal* of the I.C.S.B.S., Autumn 1982, p. 20, fig 36.
2. H. Moss. 'The Apricot Grove Studio', *Journal* of the I.C.S.B.S, Spring 1982, p. 4.

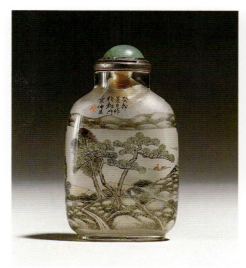
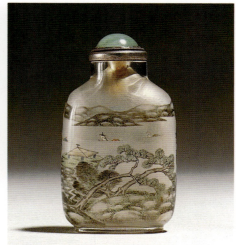

274

275

275

Rock crystal; of faceted hexagonal section, painted on the inside with a continuous scene depicting fan-tailed fish swimming amongst aquatic fronds beneath a mossy bank, signed with the date and the seal *yin*; *height: 5.7cm*.

By Ye Zhongsan the Elder; 3rd month, 1905

    PROVENANCE: C.S. Wilkinson
                   Hugh Moss

    PUBLISHED: *Journal* of the I.C.S.B.S., Autumn 1982, p. 37, fig. 92

This subject, which is first recorded in 1903, became one of the Apricot Grove Studio's most popular. The use of the faceted crystal, with its reflectivity, helps suggest the reflections one would see off the surface of the water.

The colour tone of the mossy bank is one of the most characteristic of all the Ye hues and is a vital aid in helping to distinguish their copies of the works of Zhou Leyuan from the originals.

276

276

Hair crystal; painted on the inside with a continuous scene of fan-tailed fish, partly hidden by clouds of black tourmaline needles, beneath the signature, the date and a seal; *height: 4.7cm*.

By Ye Zhongsan the Elder; 3rd month 1905

    PROVENANCE: Hugh Moss
                      The Belfort Collection

    EXHIBITED: Hong Kong Museum of Art, October, 1978
                      Arcade Chaumet, Paris, June 1982, *Catalogue*, no. 133

    PUBLISHED: Hong Kong Museum. *Catalogue*, no. 226
                      V. Jutheau. *Tabatières Chinoises*, p. 69, fig 5

A rare combination of hair crystal with inside-painting, the black tourmaline needles providing the natural effect of water reeds.

277

Rock crystal; painted on the inside with a portrait of a court official in formal dress and on the reverse with a pavilion in a mountain landscape beneath the signature, the date and a seal; *height: 6.3cm*.

By Ye Zhongsan the Elder; Mid-Autumn, 1908

    PROVENANCE: J.E.G. Byman
                      Sotheby's London, June 24th, 1975, lot 329
                      Janos Szekeres
                      Sotheby's New York, October 27th 1986, lot 227

    PUBLISHED: E.B. Curtis. *Reflected Glory in a Bottle*, colour frontispiece and p. 101, fig. 145
                      Journal of the I.C.S.B.S., Autumn 1982, p. 45, fig. 125

This remarkable bottle contains the only known portrait by Ye Zhongsan, other than one of Tan Xinbei in the Collection of Mr. and Mrs. James Li. The subject has been tentatively identified by Curtis as Dashou, the Minister of Dependencies. It is superbly painted and very much the equal of the better known portraits of Ma Shaoxuan.

This portrait differs from those of Ma in the use of colours, other than grisaille, and the subtle shading of the face, which imparts a slightly warmer flavour to it than that possessed by the more photographic portraits of Ma.

277

278

278

Chalcedony; painted on the inside with a continuous scene of fan-tailed fish amongst aquatic plants, beneath the signature, the date and a seal; *height: 5.2cm.*

By Ye Zhongsan the Elder; 2nd month, 1909

PROVENANCE: Hugh Moss
                 Heflene Collection
                 Count Kurt Blucher Von Wahlstatt

PUBLISHED: H. Moss. *Snuff Bottles of China*, p. 142, no. 381

This bottle exhibits a skillful marriage between the qualities inherent in the stone and the subject-matter. The colour and opacity of the material are evocative of murky water.

The artist has tried to mitigate the effect of a star crack in the bottle by painting the water plants in a formation which disguises the crack.

279

Rock crystal; of large size, painted on the inside with a continuous scene of one hundred boys engaged in a myriad of activities, the shoulders signed Ye Zhongsan with the date; *height: 8.8cm*.

The Ye Family at the Apricot Grove Studio; Autumn 1918

> PROVENANCE: H.G. Beasley
> Mac Beasley
> Sotheby's London, 2nd July 1984, lot 112

After 1911 the style and palette of paintings produced in the Apricot Grove Studio changed considerably. The colours became brighter, the subjects more stereotyped and the painting more often wooden.

Whilst this bottle depicts a rare subject, the features of the boys are much less individual than those depicted in the earlier schoolroom scene of 1896 (number 272).

This bottle was acquired in Beijing by H.G. Beasley on 18th July 1919, less than a year after it was painted[1].

1. Compare with the similar subject executed by Wang Xisan, number 309 below.

280

Glass; painted on the inside with a continuous scene of eight cranes clustered on a mossy bank beside a lake, framed by a pine tree, signed Ye Zhongsan with a date and seal; *height: 6.5cm*.

The Ye Family at the Apricot Grove Studio; 1930

> PROVENANCE: Hugh Moss
> Joan Wasserman

> PUBLISHED: *Journal* of the I.C.S..B.S, Autumn 1984, p. 74, fig. 215

A very fine example of a late bottle, painted by either Ye Zhongsan the Elder or Ye Xiaofeng in the early style, of a subject first recorded in 1902.

The number eight, like all even numbers, is a feminine or *yin* number. It appears in various combinations and represents the ideal number of different groups of precious, religious or mythical objects.

279

280

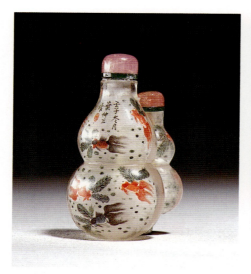
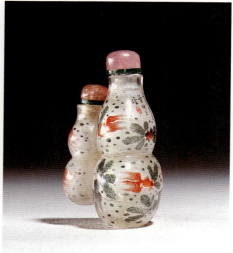

281

Rock Crystal; a double bottle, each segment of double-gourd form, painted with a continuous scene of fish amongst aquatic fronds, beneath the signature *Ye Zhongsan* and the date 1912; *height: 5.7cm.*

The Ye Family at the Apricot Grove Studio; circa 1928

    PROVENANCE: Eric Young
                       Sotheby's London, 3rd March 1987, lot 175

A small but distinctive group of bottles from this Studio exists with the date 1912[1]. Stylistically, most of these bottles bear little relation to the work which was produced in 1912 by Ye Zhongsan the Elder, whereas they are very close in style to the later works of Ye Xiaofeng and Ye Bengqi. The possibility therefore arises that this group are incorrectly dated.

The subject of fishes is more difficult because there is almost no discernable difference in the style of this subject from as early as 1903 and as late as 1925[2]. Indeed, one bottle correctly dated to 1912 is actually recorded by Moss[3].

The only major difference appears to be in the way the character 王(ren), part of the cyclical dating system, is written. On the clearly later group the top horizontal stroke does not touch the vertical stroke whereas on bottles correctly dated to 1912 the top stroke runs rather freely into the vertical stroke.

On this evidence the bottle illustrated here is likely to belong to the later group and the dating of 1928 is postulated by comparison with a set of four bottles, each with identical subject matter, illustrated by Stevens, two of which bear the wrong date of 1912 and two of which are dated, presumably correctly, to 1928[4].

1. H. Moss. 'The Apricot Grove Studio,' *Journal* of the I.C.S.B.S., Autumn 1984, p. 93.
2. H. Moss. Op. cit, *Journal* of the I.C.S.B.S, spring 1984, p. 69, fig. 199.
3. H. Moss. Op. cit, *Journal* of the I.C.S.B.S., spring 1984, p. 51, fig. 138a.
4. Bob. C. Stevens. *The Collector's Book of Snuff Bottles*, nos, 88-89.

282

Rock crystal; painted on the inside on front with numerous butterflies hovering above flowers and other plants, beneath the title, *enjoying the heavens and revelling in the earth*, the date, the signature *Shaoxuan* and the seal *Shao*, the reverse with an inscription, signature and seal; *height: 5.7cm*.

By Ma Shaoxuan; Winter 1895

    PROVENANCE: Emily Byrne Curtis
                        Sotheby's London, 2nd July 1984, lot 296

    PUBLISHED: Bob C. Stevens. *The Collector's Book of Snuff Bottles*, no. 851

The inscription on the reverse may be read as follows:

Inscription of a Hundred Butterfly painting
A hundred kinds of energy, a hundred kinds of Spring,
In a remote part of the garden, it is quiet and free from dust,
The painted flowers are as wonderful as real ones,
Not what one usually sees in a dream.

Ma Shaoxuan was one of the most prolific of all the artists in the medium. The earliest recorded of his works, signed in the name of Zhou Leyuan, is dated 1891 and the earliest recorded signed in his own name dates from 1894[1]. He appears to have painted until 1925, but the enormous variation in quality of the works signed in his name, particularly after 1912, suggests that after that date Ma enjoyed the help of a studio.

Ma was noted for his depictions of birds, animals and figures and he achieved fame with the ruling classes with his portrayal of many of the leading figures of the age in photographically realistic portraits. One of the chief characteristics of his work is the decoration of the reverse side with meticulously written inscriptions or poems.

1. H. Moss. *Chinese Snuff Bottles*. No. 2, p. 39, figs. 1 and 2.

283

Glass; an archer's ring painted on the inside with numerous butterflies hovering above flowers, beneath the inscription, *enjoying the heavens*, signed *Ma Shaoxuan* with the date and seals; *diameter: 3.8cm.*

By Ma Shaoxuan; Spring 1898

    PROVENANCE: Emily Byrne Curtis
                        Sotheby's London, 2nd July 1984, lot 296

    PUBLISHED: Bob C. Stevens. *The Collector's Book of Snuff Bottles*, no. 851

It is very rare to find objects other than snuff bottles painted by the well known artists of the medium. A vase and a pepper pot are recorded, painted by Ye Zhongsan in an attempt to widen the appeal of his works, but in general, it appears that eccentric objects were avoided.

284

Rock crystal; painted on the inside on front with The Two Sisters, Daqiao and Erqiao, seated on a cane sofa, beneath an elaborate seal, *Ma Guangjia*, the reverse with an inscription signed *Ma Shaoxuan at the Tingqinzhai (Studio for listening to the qin)*, with a date and seal *Shaoxuan*; *height: 6.8cm.*

By Ma Shaoxuan; Mid-Winter solstice, 1896

    PROVENANCE: The Belfort Collection

    PUBLISHED: V. Jutheau. *Tabatières Chinoises*, p. 69, fig. 3

    EXHIBITED: Arcade Chaumet, Paris, June 1982, *Catalogue*, no. 135

The inscription on the reverse may be partly read as follows:

The princes and ministers are in Jiangsu, praises of heroic exploits are written,
The reputation of the sisters has been increasing
Made at Listening to the Lute Studio in the Capital.

This scene from *San Guo Yan Yi (The Romance of The Three Kingdoms)*, was a popular one with Ma in his early years.
It is rare to find such an elaborate seal on one of Ma's works. This particular seal is of importance as it represents Ma's other name, Ma Guangjia (see number 294).

A copy of this subject, including a poem on the reverse, was made and signed by Ye Zhongsan the Elder in 1897[1], demonstrating how esteemed Ma had become within a very few years of his debut.

1. H. Moss. 'The Apricot Grove Studio'. *Journal* of the I.C.S.B.S., Autumn 1982, p 22, fig 41.

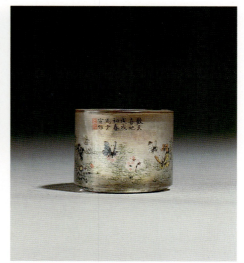

283

284

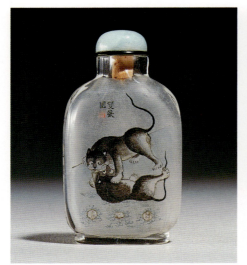

285

285

Glass; painted on the inside with two lions wrestling, beneath the inscription, *shuang huan tu (picture of double happiness)*, the reverse with a poem, signed *Ma Shaoxuan* with the date and the seal *Xuan*; *height: 6.2cm.*

By Ma Shaoxuan; Spring 1897

The poem on the reverse may be read as follows:

Beyond the mountains are more green mountains
Beyond the pavilions, more pavilions,
When will the song and dance of the West lake end?
The warm wind intoxicates the traveller
To the point that Hangzhou is mistaken for Bianzhou.
Here is written a passage from Shi Pin.

286

Glass; a miniature, painted on the inside with two wrestling lions beneath the inscription *shuang huan tu*, (picture of double happiness), the reverse with the poem *xun yin zhe bu yu, Searching for the recluse and not finding him*, by the Tang poet Jia Dao (779-843 AD), signed *Ma Shaoxuan*; with seal *Xuan*; *height: 3.7cm.*

By Ma Shaoxuan; 9th month, 1899

Miniature inside-painted snuff bottles are rare, but Ma Shaoxuan produced more of them than any of the other artists in the medium.

The poem in this case has no connection with the subject-matter of the bottle and was probably taken from a store of poems used by Ma to decorate the reverse of his works.

286

287

287

Rock crystal; painted on the inside with a scene depicting the tale of Wang Xiang, one of the twenty-four stories of filial piety, seated on the ice, beneath the inscription *wo bing qiu li (lying on the ice to look for carp)*, signed *Ma Shaoxuan*; with seals, the reverse with a cricket resting on a cabbage, beneath an inscription signed *Shaoxuan* with the seal *Shaoxuan*; *height: 6.3cm.*

By Ma Shaoxuan; undated, circa 1898

    PROVENANCE: Hugh Moss
                       Gerd Lester

    EXHIBITED: Hong Kong Museum of Art, October 1978

    PUBLISHED: H. Moss. *Chinese Snuff Bottles*, No. 2, p. 47, fig 12
                       Hong Kong Museum, *Catalogue*, no. 234

Although undated, this bottle compares with a very similar one recorded and dated 1898[1]. This is one of Ma's rarer subjects.

1. H. Moss. *Chinese Snuff Bottles*, No. 2, p. 45, where the author records that the bottle illustrated here was the first snuff bottle he ever bought.

Rock crystal; of slender form painted on each side with an extract from Wang Xizhi's Lanting Preface, the shoulders encircled by an inscription with the reign name *Guangxu 1898, copied by Ma Shaoxuan*; *height: 7cm.*

By Ma Shaoxuan; 1898

PROVENANCE:	Sigurd Larsen
	Bob Stevens
	Sotheby's New York, March 26th 1982, lot 240
	Janos Szekeres
	Sotheby's New York, October 27th 1986, lot 230
EXHIBITED:	Mikimoto Hall Tokyo, October 1978, *Catalogue*, no. 293
PUBLISHED:	Bob C. Stevens. *The Collector's Book of Snuff Bottles*, no. 840

The importance of Wang Xizhi's Lanting Preface as the finest example of Chinese calligraphy has been noted already (number 179).

Anyone who aspired to the art of calligraphy would have tried to copy the Preface in his best style and this bottle is no exception. Ma Shaoxuan is noted for the neatness of his calligraphy and on this bottle he has excelled himself with the elegant flowing brush-strokes of each character and the integrity of the whole. (Compare also with the example of the Preface by Ding Erzhong, number 251).

The inscription on the shoulders of this bottle is important because it refers to the reigning Emperor, Guangxu, (1874-1909), and thus helps to fix the cyclical dating, each double character combination of which recurs every sixty years.

289

Glass; painted on the inside with a mountain landscape and on the reverse with a poem, signed *Ma Shaoxuan*, with the date and seal *Shaoxuan*; *height: 6cm.*

By Ma Shaoxuan; 2nd month, 1900

The poem on the reverse may be read as follows:

A jade bottle buys spring,
Enjoying the rain in a thatched hut,
A gentleman sitting in the middle,
Tall bamboo all around,
White clouds are starting to form mist,
Sorrowful birds chase each other,
A sleepy lute in the green retreat,
A flying waterfall cascades from above.

The landscape on this bottle is of unusual quality for Ma Shaoxuan. It is meticulously detailed with the tiny figures in the foreground, the form of the hills is pleasing and the trees have been painted with accomplished brush-strokes.

288

289

290

Rock crystal; painted on the inside with a scene depicting The Two Sisters seated on a cane sofa, beneath the signature, a date and the seal *Shaoxuan*, the reverse with a collection of scholarly documents; *height: 6.2cm*.

By Ma Shaoxuan; Winter 1901

The subject of the scholarly documents has wrongly been called the 'contents of the waste paper basket' because of the frayed edges depicted. However, these fragments are usually copies of well known calligraphic extracts or paintings.

291

Rock crystal; of double-gourd shape, painted on the inside with an inscription, signed *Ma Shaoxuan*; with seal Shao, above a bird and flower painting and calligraphy, the reverse with a further inscription above a fan painting and calligraphy with the date inscribed; *height: 6.3cm*.

By Ma Shaoxuan; Winter 1907

Ma, in this case, has used an old rock crystal bottle of exceptional quality and has risen to the challenge by producing inscriptions and miniature paintings to match.

The top inscription on the left may be read as follows:

The heart chases the Southern clouds,
The body follows the Northern geese.
There are chrysanthemums under the gate in the old hometown,
How many flowers will bloom today?

The calligraphic rubbing reads:

The Palace of Nine Accomplishments[1].
This follows in its style.

The bird and flower painting is signed *Ba Da Shan Ren*, (the painter Zhu Da, 1625- c. 1705).

The calligraphic painting on.the lower bulb of the reverse reads:

On the mountain ahead, the wind and the rain are cold.
I rest my horse and sit under the weeping willow.
Where do the cassia flowers fall?
In the Southern gulley, the autumn waters are fragrant.

1. The Palace of Nine Accomplishments was originally a Tang Dynasty Imperial summer retreat in Shaanxi Province. The statesman Wei Zheng (580-643) compiled a work called Inscriptions of the Palace of Nine Accomplishments, which was written out by the famous calligrapher, Quyang Xun (557-641) and subsequently carved on a stele.
Although the Palace no longer survives, the stele has come down through history as a model of Kaishu, standard block writing.

290

291

292

Glass; painted on the inside with Huang Chenyen riding a mule in a snowy landscape towards a bridge, followed by a small boy with a double-gourd across his back, signed *Shaoxuan* with seal *Shao*, the reverse with a lengthy poem, signed *Ma Shaoxuan*, seal *Shaoxuan*; *height: 5.9cm*.

By Ma Shaoxuan; undated, circa 1910-1912

    PROVENANCE: Gerd Lester

The poem on the reverse may be read as follows:

All night the North wind blows,
The red clouds thicken across 10,000 miles,
The snow flies chaotically in the vast expanse,
Completely changing the appearance of the landscape,
Raising one's head to look at the extreme void
One suspects that it is two dragons fighting.
Riding a mule across the small bridge,
Sighing to solitude about the frailty of the plum blossoms.

This is a rare subject for Ma Shaoxuan, although commonly found on bottles from the Apricot Grove Studio of the Ye Family. It is treated on this bottle with the delicacy which characterises Ma's best figure painting. An almost identical bottle, dated to 1911, is illustrated by Moss in *Chinese Snuff Bottles*, No. 2, p. 19, col. pl. E.

293

Glass; painted on the inside with a portrait of a court official and on the reverse with a poem, signed *Ma Shaoxuan*, with the seal *Shaoxuan* and the date; *height: 6cm*.

By Ma Shaoxuan; 10th month 1902

The poem on the reverse may be read:

Ice is crystal clear, and jade is clean and pure,
But there is still something else:
When entering the Fragrance land
All that is dyed black will not be dark.

Ma Shaoxuan is renowned for the series of portraits of leading Qing Dynasty figures which he executed between 1900 and 1915. These portraits are technically brilliant, each rendered with almost photographic exactitude in a uniform grisaille palette. They are rare and less than fifty have been recorded.

292

293

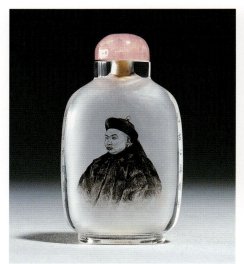

294

294

Rock crystal; painted on the inside with a portrait of a court official, the reverse with a poem, signed *Shaoxuan di Ma Guangjia*, with seal *Shaoxuan* and the date, together with a second inscription *Xiechen da Xiong ren da ren Zheng (For the approval of brother Ren Xiechen); height: 6.2cm.*

By Ma Shaoxuan; undated, circa 1900-1910

PROVENANCE: Edmund Dwyer
                   Hugh Moss

EXHIBITED: Hong Kong Museum of Art, October 1978

PUBLISHED: Hong Kong Museum. *Catalogue*, no. 235
                  E.B. Curtis. *Reflected Glory in a Bottle*, p. 95, fig 132
                  Journal of the I.C.S.B.S., June 1981, p. 37, fig 14, and Summer 1986, back cover

The poem on the reverse may be read:

Embracing the classics, accomplished of talent,
Enjoying wealth and popularity,
Magnanimous of will,
Calm of spirit,
Basing friendships on virtuous principles,
Prudent and dignified,
Venerable of appearance, venerable of mind,
A brilliant man, this nobleman.

The middle character, *di*, in the signature on this bottle originally led to some confusion. Di may mean 'younger brother' or it may be used as a term of respect meaning 'to act in a submissive manner as a younger brother should'[1].

In this case it was originally thought that the bottle was signed by younger brother, Ma Guangjia[2]. However, when the character, *di*, is used as a term of respect, when dedicating a work of art to a person of superior position, it was common for the artist to sign first his art name, followed by *di*, followed by his real name.

295

This bottle, judging by the tone of the poem is clearly dedicated to a person of high standing. The character, *di*, may therefore be assumed to be used as a term of respect. This, together with the use of the seal *Shaoxuan*, points towards the bottle being by Ma Shaoxuan, who reveals his true name, Ma Guangjia[2].

Xiechen, to whom the bottle is dedicated, was the *zi* of Sun Jiania, (1827-1909), an important offiical of the Qing Dynasty[3].

1. H. Moss. *Journal* of the I.C.S.B.S., June 1981, p. 38.
2. See also number 284 above, which has the seal, Ma Guangjia.
3. H. Moss. *Journal* of the I.C.S.B.S., Summer 1986, back cover.

295

Glass; painted on the inside with a portrait of an unknown official, the reverse with a poem, *signed Ma Shaoxuan*, with the seal *Shaoxuan* and the date; *height: 6.3cm.*

By Ma Shaoxuan; Mid-Summer 1905

PROVENANCE: Lilla Perry
Bob C. Stevens
Sotheby's New York, 26th March 1982, lot 216
The Meiling Collection
Sotheby's New York, 15th March 1984, lot 200

EXHIBITED: Mikimoto Hall, Tokyo, October 1978, *Catalogue*, no. 290

PUBLISHED: Bob C. Stevens. *The Collector's Book of Snuff Bottles*, no. 845
Lilla S. Perry. *Chinese Snuff Bottles*, p. 136, fig. 2
Emily Byrne Curtis. *Reflected Glory in a Bottle*, p. 99, fig. 140/141, where a translation of the poem is given
Journal of the I.C.S.B.S., December 1978, p. 136, no. 134
Arts of Asia, Jan.-Feb. 1982, p. 94, no. 9

296

296

Glass; painted on the inside with a portrait of Liang Dunyen, the reverse undecorated; *height: 6.4cm.*

Attributed to Ma Shaoxuan; circa 1900-1915

PROVENANCE: Dr. and Mrs. Louis Wolferz
                          Sotheby's New York, 3rd October 1980, lot 125

PUBLISHED: E.B. Curtis, *Reflected glory in a Bottle*, p. 15 fig. 20

Although this bottle is unsigned, the style of painting places it unmistakably as a work of Ma Shaoxuan. Several of Ma's portraits exist without any signature or calligraphy on the reverse and the reason for this lack is not known. One possibility is that the order was cancelled, before completion, for some unknown reason.

Liang was one of a group of upper-class Chinese boys sent to the United States in 1872 for education, and later became a diplomat.

297

Rock crystal; painted on the inside with a portrait, of General Jiang Yenxing, the reverse with a poem, a respectful dedication *for the pleasure of General Binchen, my brother*, and the seal *Shaoxuan*; *height: 5.7cm.*

By Ma Shaoxuan; circa 1900-1915

PROVENANCE: Lilla Perry
                          Hugh Moss
                          The Belfort Collection

EXHIBITED: Arcade Chaumet, Paris, June 1982, *Catalogue*, no. 136

PUBLISHED: Lilla S. Perry. *Chinese Snuff Bottles*, p. 136, fig. 135
                          E.B. Curtis. *Reflected Glory in a Bottle*, p. 74, fig. 100, where the poem on the reverse is translated
                          V. Jutheau. *Tabatières Chinoises*, p. 70, fig 1

Although unsigned, the seal, *Shaoxuan*, the style of the calligraphy and of the portrait itself, all point clearly to Ma Shaoxuan as the artist in this case. This bottle also compares very closely to the signed example, number 298 below.

A third portrait of an officer was exhibited at the Hong Kong Museum of Art, October 1978, *Catalogue*, no. 237.

297

298

298

Rock crystal; painted on the inside with a portrait of an officer, the reverse with a poem, signed *Ma Shaoxuan*, seal *Shaoxuan*; *height: 6.2cm*.

By Ma Shaoxuan; circa 1900-1915

    PROVENANCE: Sotheby's New York, 1st July 1985, lot 177

    PUBLISHED: E. B. Curtis. *Journal* of the I.C.S.B.S., Autumn 1985, p. 133, fig 8

The inscription on the reverse of this bottle is dedicated to Tie Hou.

The poem may be read as follows:

Chaste virtue through and through,
Clear and honest of ambition,
Clear and transparent both inside and out,
The glory of the nation.

Emily Byrne Curtis has identified the portrait on this bottle as that of Colonel Zhang Lanzhuan.

299

Glass; painted on the inside with a portrait of the actor Tan Xinbei in his role as Qin Qiong in Mai Ma[1], the reverse with a poem, signed *Ma Shaoxuan*, with *seal Shaoxuan*; *height: 6.3cm*.

By Ma Shaoxuan; circa 1900

This is a superb and very rare portrait of the actor Tan Xinbei in an unusual role. Several portraits of Tan exist in his role as General Huang Zhong, mostly dated around 1900, when the actor was at the peak of his popularity, but only a handful of portraits exist of him in other roles or costumes. The addition of colours to the face in this portrait is noteworthy when compared to the previous group of portraits, but is a trait followed by Ma in each of his portraits of the actor.

Tan was born in 1846 and died in 1917 and was known as the "little hailer to the heavens". He was a favourite of the Empress Dowager[2].

1. E.B. Curtis. *Reflected Glory in a Bottle*, p. 85, fig 112.
2. E.B. Curtis citing A.C. Scott. *The Classical Theatre of China*. London, Allan & Unwin Ltd, 1957.

300

Glass; painted on the inside with a portrait of Tan Xinbei in his role as General Huang Zhong, the reverse with a hen and its chicks on a mossy bank beneath sprays of willow, *signed Zi Yici*, with the date; *height: 7cm*.

By Zi Yici; Summer, 1901

PROVENANCE: Sigurd Larsen
Bob C. Stevens
Sotheby's New York, 26th March 1982, lot 219
Meiling Collection
Sotheby's New York, 15th March 1984, lot 203

EXHIBITED: Mikimoto Hall, Tokyo, October, 1978, *Catalogue*, no. 299

PUBLISHED: Bob C. Stevens. *The Collector's Book of Snuff Bottles*, no. 874

This artist, one of the finest in the medium is one of the rarest and few of his works have been recorded. He appears to have worked in Beijing from 1899 to 1907.

Zi was particularly fine as a portrait painter. His portraits are warmer and softer than those of Ma Shaoxuan, with broad brush-strokes and plenty of shaded wash, rather than the pencilled technique of Ma. The quality of Zi's brushwork on the reverse side of this bottle is particularly accomplished in the treatment of the hen's tail feathers, the spray of willow and the mossy bank itself.

299

300

301

301

Glass; painted on the inside with a portrait of a bald-headed man, Prince Qing, and on the reverse with a portrait of Li Hongzhang in court dress; *height: 6.7cm.*

By Zi Yici; circa 1899-1907

PROVENANCE: Dr. N.C. Shen
Emily Byrne Curtis

PUBLISHED: E.B. Curtis. *Journal* of the I.C.S.B.S., p. 132, fig 5

Zi Yici painted a number of portraits, mostly unsigned, which are each very similar in their style and conception. Each is contained within an oval frame with a black or grey background and each is painted with warmth and sympathy, in the soft shaded style apparent in the preceding portrait of Tan Xinbei.

One of this very distinctive group is signed with Zi Yici's signature[1], and other unsigned examples are illustrated by H. Moss in *Snuff Bottles of China*, p. 149, no 409 and in *Chinese Snuff Bottles* No. 5, p. 36, fig 36

The latter snuff bottle also contains a portrait of Li Hongzheng. Li and Prince Qing were two of the Dowager Empress Cixi's chief advisers and they had the task of negotiating a settlement after the Boxer uprising in 1900.

1. In the Collection of Mr. and Mrs. James Li, illustrated, cover of the *Journal* of the I.C.S.B.S., Autumn, 1987.

302

Rock crystal; painted on the inside with a continuous scene depicting a tree overhanging a mossy bank with fish swimming below in a pond, the shoulders with an inscription *tai wang shi qingbi (penned by Tai Wang Shi Qing)* signed *Zi Yici zuo yu Jingmen (Zi Yici made this at Jingmen)*, with the date and seal *yin*; *height: 6cm.*

By Zi Yici; 8th month, 1907

With this work Zi Yici shows himself the equal of Zhou Leyuan in his control of composition and brush-work. The trunk of the tree is particularly well painted in its use of brush-strokes without outline and the shading of the mossy bank is achieved with the utmost skill.

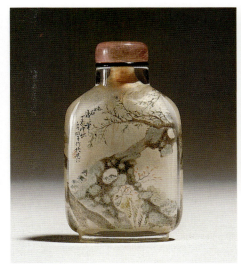
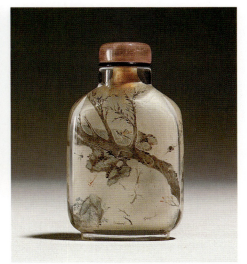

302

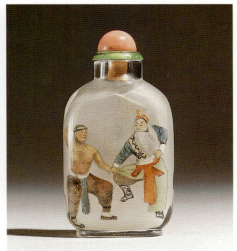

303

303

Glass; painted on the inside with a European solider riding a horse and on the reverse with a scene from the Opera 'The Lucky Pearl', depicting Xizo En challenging the boxer Jiao; *height: 6.5cm*.

Unsigned but attributed to Zi Yici; circa 1900

    PROVENANCE: Mr. and Mrs. P. Bozzo

    PUBLISHED: *Journal* of the I.C.S.B.S., Autumn 1986, p. 24, fig 3

E.B. Curtis has discovered a bottle with this subject, signed by Zi Yici, in the Ashmolean Museum, Oxford, which allows the attribution of this bottle to the artist[1].

The bottle was possibly painted around the time of the Boxer uprising in 1900 when there would have been large numbers of European troops in Peking.

1. E.B. Curtis. *Journal* of the I.C.S.B.S., Autumn 1986, p. 24.

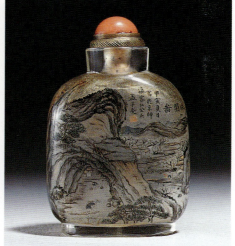

304

304

Glass; painted on the inside with a portrait of Zhang Zuolin, the 'Mukdin Tiger', and on the reverse with a mountain landscape, with an inscription signed *Meng Zishou*; and dated; *height: 6.3cm.*

By Meng Zishou; Summer, 1914

    PROVENANCE: Emily Byrne Curtis
                       Sotheby's New York, 1st July 1985, lot 176

    PUBLISHED: E.B. Curtis. *Reflected Glory in a Bottle*, p. 78/79, figs. 102 and 104

The inscription on the reverse may be read:

Painting of Peach Blossom Spring
Written at the Capital
For the approval of Bengong of Yingke

Meng Zishou's recorded works date from 1904-1919. He was an artist whose work varied in quality from very fine to poor and this has resulted in his being held in undeservedly low regard.

Nevertheless, his best work, as in this bottle and in another portrait bottle in the O'Dell Collection[1], is of exceptional quality. The portrait is treated with sensitivity and the landscape scene on the reverse is well constructed with substantial vitality.

1. John G. Ford. *Chinese Snuff Bottles. The Edward Choate O'Dell Collection, Catalogue*, no. 189.

305

Rock crystal; a miniature bottle painted on the interior with Tan Xinbei in an operatic role, the reverse with a horse in a landscape, signed *Meng Zishou; height: 4.2cm.*

By Meng Zishou; undated, circa 1914-1919

One of very few miniature bottles recorded by this artist, and the only one known containing a portrait, by any artist.

Despite the small size, the portrait is finely executed, with the figure exhibiting a similar depth of expression as that of the preceding bottle. The scene on the reverse is rather wooden and an example of the slightly eratic quality of Meng.

305

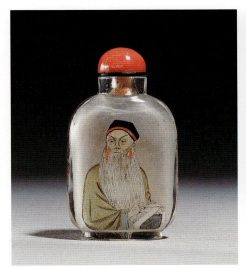
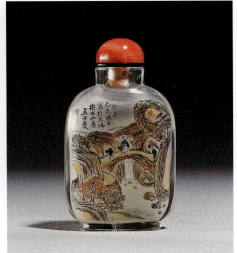

306

306

Glass; painted on the inside with a portrait of Tan Xinbei in one of his operatic roles, the reverse with figures crossing a natural bridge in a mountain landscape beneath the title *ji zi* (*Sending of the Son*), and an inscription, *Written at the Capital at the Enjoy Tradition Mountain Retreat*, signed *Meng Zishou*; *height: 5.7cm.*

By Meng Zishou; Autumn, 1919

A very rare portrait by Meng of the actor, Tan Xinbei. The poise of the figure and the overall control of the painting compare very well with the similar subjects executed by Ma Shaoxuan and Zi Yici. As in the preceding bottle, the landscape has vigour and vitality.

307

Glass; painted on the inside with scenes depicting mounted Manchu hunting geese, signed *Sun Xingwu*, with seals and the date; *height: 6.1cm*.

By Sun Xingwu; Summer 1899

An artist whose works are difficult to find, with the recorded examples dating from 1894-1900. Sun was a skilled painter who favoured the type of action scenes depicted on this bottle. He often signed his name in archaistic style.

308

Rock crystal; painted on the inside with two pandas in a bamboo grove beneath the inscription *Wang Xisan made this at Taipingzhuang, Jingzi, seal Xisan*, the reverse with two monkeys beside a fast-flowing stream looking towards a third monkey in a pine tree; *height: 6.9cm*.

By Wang Xisan; Winter, 1962

Wang Xisan was born in 1938 and was taught the art of painting inside snuff bottles by the two surviving sons of Ye Zhongsen, Ye Xiaofeng and Ye Benqi, whose Beijing Studio was re-established in 1954.

Wang began painting in 1958 and whilst his early works are very similar in style to those of his masters, by 1960 he had begun to experiment with new subjects and styles. His work during this decade in Beijing exhibited imagination and increasing skill and he became a worthy successor to the great artists of the Beijing School of the turn of the century.

This bottle still shows traces of the style of the Ye brothers, particularly in the execution of the grass where a green wash is first painted and a blunt instrument is then scored against this to impose the detail[1]. The subject-matter, however, with its freshness and vitality, marks a radical departure from the work of the Ye Brothers who continued to paint designs to which they had become accustomed.

1. H. Moss. *Journal* of the I.C.S.B.S., June 1981, p. 33.

307

308

309

Rock crystal; painted on the inside with a continuous scene of one hundred boys playing various games in a garden, beneath an inscription and the title *Bai Zi Tu (Hundred Boys Drawing)*, the date and the seal *Xisan*; *height: 6.8cm*.

By Wang Xisan; 1968

    PROVENANCE: Ann Cohen
                      Hugh Moss

    PUBLISHED: *Journal* of the I.C.S.B.S., Summer 1984, p. 21, fig 1

The inscription may be read:

Inside-painted hundred boys drawings are as rare as unicorn horns.
I have just laboured unremittingly for twenty-one days
To bring to completion
The finest work in my career.

As Wang was clearly very proud of this work it is unclear why he did not sign it other than with his seal. It is possible that with the cultural revolution in full swing he felt it prudent not to do so, in common with other artists of the time.

Wang Xisan himself recollects that he had always wished to paint this subject which had been previously executed by the Ye Family[1]. During the cultural revolution he was sent to Hebei, and after studying the children of the local school he worked non-stop for twenty-one days to achieve the painting[2].

1. See the Ye example, number 279 above.
2. *Journal* of the I.C.S.B.S., Summer 1984, p. 21.

310

Glass; painted on the inside, *after Castiglione*, with two of the Emperor's favourite dogs, one, 'with golden wings', scratching its ear, beneath the seal *Wang Xisan*, the other, 'striped like a tiger', seated beside a rock beneath the inscription *Yi hu Zhai (One Bottle Studio)*; *height: 6.1cm*.

By Wang Xisan; 1969

    PROVENANCE: Hugh Moss
                      Robert Hall
                      R. Galpine
                      Sotheby's London, 6th May 1986, lot 285

In 1969 Wang began signing his works in Peking at the One Bottle Studio. In 1973 he moved to Fucheng and established another Studio under Government Supervision. During the following years the studio produced many works of variable quality with the signature of Wang Xisan, some of which were by his pupils. Whilst Wang re-assumed control of the output in 1977, his later works, perhaps because of the commercial pressures put upon him, have tended to be stiffer and more stereo-typed, and have lost some of the vitality and originality of the pre-1970 works.

This bottle, however, dating from 1969, is one of Wang's masterpieces. Whilst it is a copy of two of the best known paintings by the great 18th century Jesuit artist, Castiglione (1688-1766) and therefore might be called unoriginal, the perfection of the reproduction is such as to astound and lift the bottle from the level of superb craftsmanship to the status of a true work of art. The use of the amber-coloured glass to simulate the silk background of the originals is a final touch[1].

With its recollection of the height of Imperial Chinese taste of the eighteenth century, when many of the greatest snuff bottles were made, and its manifest demonstration of the heights to which a modern snuff bottle can aspire, no other bottle could be better suited to round off this Exhibition.

1. The originals are illustrated by Cécile and Michel Beurdeley, *Giuseppe Castiglione: A Jesuit Painter at the Court of the Chinese Emperors*, p. 175, no. 61 and p. 176, no. 67.

309

310

Selected Bibliography

Ayers, John, 'Chinese Glass' in *Arts of the Ch'ing Dynasty*, pp. 17-27. London Oriental Ceramic Society, 1965

Beurdeley, Cécile and Michel. *Giuseppe Castiglione: A Jesuit Painter at the Court of the Chinese Emperors*. Translated by Michael Bullock, Rutland, Vermont and Tokyo: Tuttle, 1977

Beurdeley, Michel and Marie Therese Lambert-Brouillet. *L'Eunuque aux Trois Joyaux*. Office du Livre, S.A., Fribourg, Switzerland, 1984

Bartholomew, Terese Tse. *I-Hsing Ware*. China Institure in America. New York, 1977

Chang, Lin-sheng. 'Painted Enamel Snuff Bottles of the Ch'ing Dynasty'. *Journal* of the International Chinese Snuff Bottle Society, March 1979, pp. 4-12 and 37-39

Chinese Exhibition at Burlington House in 1935-36. Faber and Faber, London, 1936

Chinese Jades Throughout the Ages, a definitive catalogue in *Transactions of the Oriental Ceramic Society*, Vol. 41, 1976

Curtis, Emily Byrne. *Reflected Glory in a Bottle: Chinese Snuff Bottle Portraits*. New York: Soho Bodhi, 1980

Curtis, Emily Byrne. 'The Impact of the West — Part One, China in the Nineteenth Century'. *Journal* of the International Chinese Snuff Bottle Society, June 1981, pp. 5-12

d'Argencé, R.Y.L. (ed.) *Treasures from Shanghai Museum: 6,000 Years of Chinese Art*. Shanghai Museum and the Asian Art Museum of San Francisco, 1983

Fong Wen (ed.). *The Great Bronze Age of China*. Thames and Hudson, London, 1980

Ford, John G. *Chinese Snuff Bottles. The Edward Choate O'Dell Collection*. The Asia House Gallery, New York City, November 1982

Garner, Sir Harry M. *Chinese and Japanese Cloisonné Enamels*. Faber and Faber, London, 1962

Garner, Sir Harry M. *Chinese Lacquer*. Faber and Faber, 1979

Gillingham, M. *Chinese Painted Enamels*, Ashmolean Museum, Oxford, 1978

Hansford, S. Howard. *Chinese Carved Jades*. Faber and Faber, London, 1968

Hardy, Sheila Yorke. 'Ku Yueh Hsüan — A New Hypothesis', *Oriental Art*, Winter 1949-50, pp. 116-25

Hong Kong Museum of Art. *'Chinese Snuff Bottles'*, *Catalogue*, October/November 1977

Hong Kong Museum of Art. *'Snuff Bottles of the Ch'ing Dynasty'*, *Catalogue*, October/December 1978, by G. Tsang and H.M. Moss

Hummel, Arthur W. (ed.). *Eminent Chinese of the Ch'ing Period*. Government Printing Office, Washington, 1943-1944

Illustrated Catalogue of Ancient Jade Artefacts in the National Palace Museum. Taipei, 1982

Illustrated Catalogue of Ch'ing Dynasty Porcelain in the National Palace Museum, Republic of China, Vol. 1 (Kang hsi and Yung Cheng ware); Vol. 2 (Ch'ien Lung ware and other wares).

Ip Yee. *Chinese Jade Carving*. Hong Kong Museum of Art, 1983

Ip Yee and Laurence C.S. Tam. *Chinese Bamboo Carving*. Hong Kong Museum of Art, Vol. 1, 1978, Vol. 2, 1982

Jenyns, Soame. *Chinese Art: The Minor Arts II*, Vol. IV. Oldbourne Press, London, 1965

Jenyns, Soame. *Later Chinese Porcelain*. Faber and Faber, 1971

Journal of the International Chinese Snuff Bottle Society (referred to as *Journal* of the ICSBS)

Jutheau, Viviane. *Tabatières Chinoises*. Denoel, Paris, 1980

Lady David. *Illustrated Catalogue of Ch'ing Enamelled Ware in the Percival David Foundation of Chinese Art*. London, 1973

Masterpieces of Chinese Enamelled Ware in the National Palace Museum, Taipei, 1971

Masterpieces of Chinese Snuff Bottles in the National Palace Museum. Taipei, 1974

Medley, Margaret. *The Chinese Potter: A Practical History of Chinese Ceramics*. Phaidon Press Ltd., Oxford, 1976

Moss, Hugh M. *Chinese Snuff Bottles of the Silica or Quartz Group*. London: Bibelot, 1971

Moss, Hugh M. *Snuff Bottles of China*. London: Bibelot, 1971

Moss, Hugh M. *By Imperial Command: An Introduction to Ch'ing Imperial Painted Enamels.* Hong Kong, Hibiya Co. Ltd., 1976

Moss, Hugh M. (ed.). *Chinese Snuff Bottles*, No. 1, 1963; No. 2, 1964; No. 3, 1965; No. 4. 1966; No. 5, 1969; No. 6, 1974

Moss, Hugh M. 'An Imperial Habit — Part I'. *Journal* of the International Chinese Snuff Bottle Society, December 1975, pp. 3-15

Moss, Hugh M. 'An Imperial Habit — Part II'. *Journal* of the International Chinese Snuff Bottle Society, March 1976, pp. 12-21

Moss, Hugh M. 'Enamelled Glass Wares of the Ku Yueh Hsüan Group'. *Journal* of the International Chinese Snuff Bottle Society, June 1978, pp 5-25

Moss, Hugh M. 'European Influence on the Ch'ing Imperial Workshop', Connoisseur, January 1975, pp. 41-45. Reprinted in *Journal* of the International Chinese Snuff Bottle Society, March 1979, pp. 25-29

Moss, Hugh M. 'The Apricot Grove Studio. The Ye Family of Snuff Bottle Artists'. *Journal* of the International Chinese Snuff Bottle Society, Spring 1982, pp. 1-8

Moss, Paul. *Documentary Chinese Works of Art in Scholars' Taste*. Sydney L. Moss Ltd., London, 1983

Moss, Paul. *Emperor, Scholar, Artisan, Monk; The Creative Personality in Chinese Works of Art*. Sydney L. Moss Ltd., London, 1984

Moss, Paul. *The Literati Mode: Chinese Scholar Paintings, Calligraphy and Desk Objects*. Sydney L. Moss Ltd., London, 1986

National Palace Museum, Taiwan. *Special Exhibition of Chinese Lacquer in the Palace Museum Collection*, 1981

Perry, Lilla S. *Chinese Snuff Bottles; The Adventures and Studies of a Collector*. Rutland, Vermont and Tokyo: Tuttle, 1960

Spence, Jonathan, D. *Emperor of China; Self-Portrait of K'ang-hsi*. Alfred A. Knopf, New York, 1974

Stevens, Bob. *The Collector's Book of Snuff Bottles*. John Weatherhill Inc., New York, 1976

Tsang, Gerard and H. M. Moss. *Chinese Decorated Gourds*, in *International Asian Antiques Fair Catalogue*. Andamans East International Ltd., Hong Kong, 1983

Tsang, Gerard C.C. *Chinese Snuff Bottles*. Hong Kong Museum of Art, 1977. Catalogue of an Exhibition held October 15-November 26, 1977.

Tsang, Gerard and H. M. Moss. *Snuff Bottles of the Ch'ing Dynasty*. Hong Kong Museum of Art, 1978

G. Tsang and H.M. Moss, *Arts from the Scholar's Studio*, Oriental Ceramic Society of Hong Kong, 1986

Wan Yi (Chief Compiler). *Life in the Forbidden City*. The Commercial Press Ltd., Hong Kong, 1983

Watt, James C. Y. *Chinese Jades from Han to Ch'ing*. The Asia Society, New York, 1980

Weng Wan-go. *Chinese Painting and Calligraphy: A Pictorial Survey*. New York 1978

Weng Wan-go and Yang Boda. *The Palace Museum Peking: Treasures from the Forbidden City*. Orbis Publishing, London, 1982

Werner, E.T.C. *A Dictionary of Chinese Mythology*. The Julian Press, New York, 1961

Williams, C.A.S. *Outlines of Chinese Symbolism and Art Motives*. Kelly and Walsh, Shanghai, 1941

Wills, G. *Jade of the East*. John Weatherhill Inc., New York, 1972

Yang, Boda. *Tributes From Guangdong to the Qing Court*. Catalogue of a Joint Exhibition by the Palace Museum Beijing and The Art Gallery, The Chinese University of Hong Kong. Don Basco Printing Co., Hong Kong, 1987